Check you know it all with CGP!

Quick question — do you own CGP's
Knowledge Organiser for AQA GCSE French?

You do? Très bien! Now you can use this Knowledge Retriever
to check you've got everything stuck in your brain.

There are memory tests for each topic, plus mixed quiz questions
to make extra sure you've really remembered all the crucial points. Enjoy.

CGP — still the best! ☺

Our sole aim here at CGP is to produce the highest quality books —
carefully written, immaculately presented and dangerously close to being funny.

Then we work our socks off to get them out to you
— at the cheapest possible prices.

Contents

Topic 9 — Travel and Tourism

Topic 10 — Current and Future Study and Employment

Topic 11 — Grammar

Published by CGP.
Editors: Keith Blackhall, Eleanor Claringbold, Matt Topping.
Contributors: Marie-Laure Delvallée, Sophie Desgland, Jackie Shaw, Sarah Sweeney.

ISBN: 978 1 78908 719 2

With thanks to Hannah Roscoe for the proofreading.
With thanks to Lottie Edwards for the copyright research.

Printed by Elanders Ltd, Newcastle upon Tyne.
Clipart from Corel®

Based on the classic CGP style created by Richard Parsons

How to Use This Book

Every page in this book has a matching page in the GCSE French **Knowledge Organiser**. Before using this book, try to **memorise** everything on a Knowledge Organiser page. Then follow these **seven steps** to see how much knowledge you're able to retrieve...

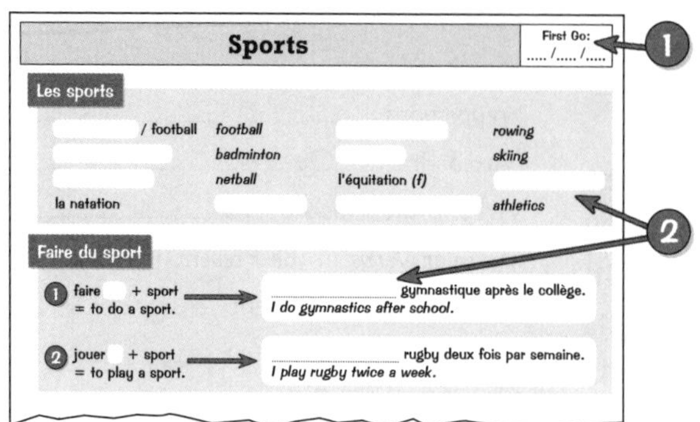

1. In this book, there are two versions of each page. Find the **'First Go'** of the page you've tried to memorise, and write the **date** at the top.

2. Use what you've learned from the Knowledge Organiser to **fill in** any dotted lines or white spaces.

3. Use the Knowledge Organiser to **check your work**. Use a **different coloured pen** to write in anything you missed or that wasn't quite right. This lets you see clearly what you **know** and what you **don't know**.

4. After doing the 'First Go' page, **wait a few days**. This is important because **spacing out** your retrieval practice helps you to remember things better.

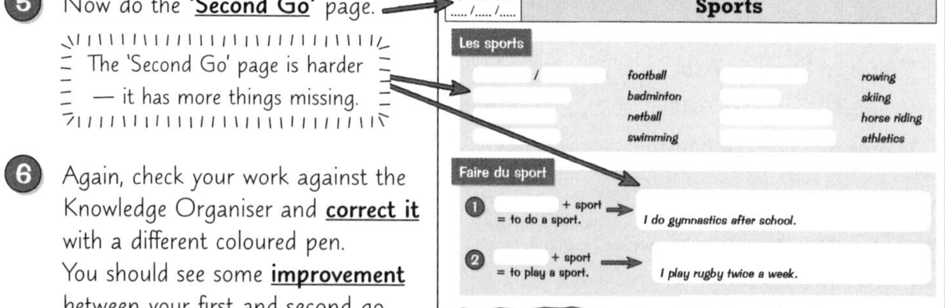

5. Now do the **'Second Go'** page.

   The 'Second Go' page is harder — it has more things missing.

6. Again, check your work against the Knowledge Organiser and **correct it** with a different coloured pen. You should see some **improvement** between your first and second go.

7. **Wait** another few days, then try recreating the whole Knowledge Organiser page on a **blank piece of paper**. If you can do this, you'll know you've **really learned it**.

There are also **Mixed Practice Quizzes** dotted throughout the book:

- The quizzes come in sets of four. They test a mix of content from the previous few pages.
- Do each quiz on a different day — write the date you do each one at the top of the quiz.
- Tick the questions you get right and record your score in the box at the end.

Numbers

First Go: ..... /..... /.....

Un, deux, trois

.... vingt-sept

43

.... deux mille douze

.... cent quatre-vingt-quatorze

456

Il y a .... garçons et .... filles.
.... *twenty-one boys and twenty-one girls.*

For feminine nouns, use '.........'.

Je suis né en ....
.... *in 1996.*

Le château coûte .... d'euros.
.... *costs eight million euros.*

À vendre

Premier, deuxième, troisième

premier / première		sixième	
	2nd		*7th*
	3rd		*8th*
	4th	neuvième	
cinquième			*10th*

J'en prends .... s'il vous plaît.
.... *a dozen please.*

Elle n'a qu' .... de bonbons.
She .... *has about ten sweets.*

Il y avait .... de gâteaux.
There were about twenty ....*.*

Il a lu .... de livres.
He read lots of ....*.*

.... voyages en train a augmenté.
The number of journeys by train ....*.*

Second Go:
..... /..... /.....

Numbers

Un, deux, trois

There are twenty-one boys and twenty-one girls.

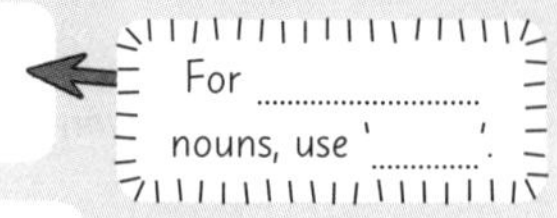

I was born in 1996.

The castle costs eight million euros.

Premier, deuxième, troisième

/ *1st*

2nd

3rd

4th

5th

6th

7th

8th

9th

10th

I'll have a dozen please.

She only has about ten sweets.

There were about twenty cakes.

He read lots of books.

The number of journeys by train has increased.

Times and Dates

First Go: ..... /..... /.....

Quelle heure est-il?

Il est heures.

Il est heures .

Il est heures et .

Il est heures .

Il est ... ...de l'après-midi.	It is 3:12... ...in the morning. ...in .
Il est neuf heures moins dix .	It is in the evening.
Il est vingt heures trente et un.	It is .

Les jours de la semaine

lundi

mercredi

samedi

Use '.........' to say something happens on a certain day.

le lundi ....

Les mois de l'année

juillet

février

septembre

avril

décembre

C'est quand?

this evening

cet après-midi

the day after tomorrow

the day before yesterday

demain *tomorrow morning*

le lendemain

la semaine prochaine

le week-end dernier

always

sometimes

(assez) souvent

(quite)

rarely

Quelle est la date ....?
What is .... today?

C'est ....
It's the fifteenth of May.

Second Go:
..... /..... /.....

Times and Dates

Quelle heure est-il?

	It is 3:12... ...in the morning. ...in the afternoon.
	It is 8:50 in the evening.
	It is 20:31.

Les jours de la semaine

on Mondays

Les mois de l'année

C'est quand?

this evening
this afternoon
the day after tomorrow
the day before yesterday
tomorrow morning
the next day

next week
last weekend
always
sometimes
(quite) often
rarely

What is the date today?

It's the fifteenth of May.

Questions

First Go: ..... /..... /.....

Les mots interrogatifs

_______ when? _______ how? _______ what?

pourquoi? _______ _______ how much / many? que? _______

_______ where? qui? _______ quel? _______

.... femmes aiment chanter?
Which women like ....?

'Quel' .... with the noun:
'quel' (....................), 'quels' (....................),
'quelle' (....................), 'quelles' (....................)

Three ways to ask questions

1. Change your _______ _______ — make your voice go _______ at the end of a _______.

   .... faim?
   Are you hungry?

   Use '........' to answer 'yes' to a negative question.

2. Use '_______' for 'yes' or 'no' questions...

   .... tu aimes jouer au tennis?
   Do you like ....?

   ...or '_______' for questions starting with '_______'.

   .... tu fais dans ton temps libre?
   What do you do in your ....?

3. _______ the verb and subject around and add a _______.

   .... du sport?
   Do you do any sport?

Common questions

C'est ....?
What colour is it?

....................?
What is it?

À ....?
At what time?

Ça s'écrit ....?
How is that written?

Pour ....?
For how long?

C'est ....?
What day is it?

C'est ....?
How much is it?

.... viens tu?
Where are you from?

Que ....?
What does ... mean?

Second Go: ..... /..... /.....

Questions

Les mots interrogatifs

when?

why?

where?

how?

how much / many?

who?

what?

what?

which?

Which women like singing?

'Quel' .... with the ....:
'..........' (masc. sing.), '..........' (masc. pl.),
'..........' (fem. sing.), '..........' (fem. pl.)

Three ways to ask questions

1. Change your — make your .

Are you hungry?

Use '......' to answer 'yes' to a ....

2. Use for questions...

Do you like playing tennis?

...or for starting .

What do you do in your free time?

3. Swap around and .

Do you do any sport?

Common questions

What colour is it?

What is it?

At what time?

How is that written?

For how long?

What day is it?

How much is it?

Where are you from?

What does ... mean?

Being Polite

First Go: ..... /..... /.....

Bonjour...au revoir

	hello (on phone)		*Have a good trip!*
bienvenue		Bonne chance!	
	good night	de rien	
	see you soon		*OK*
à tout à l'heure		quel dommage	
	see you tomorrow	je suis désolé(e)	

Comment ça va?

.... Sylvie, comment ça va?
Hi Sylvie, ...?

Bonsoir! ...., ...?
....! *I'm fine, and you?*

Je .... merci beaucoup.
I feel good ....

.... te présenter Marc?
May I .... Marc?

....
Pleased to meet you.

	How are you? (form.)		*Super!*
comme ci, comme ça		pas mal	
Ça ne va pas bien.			*And you? (form.)*
	I don't know.		*This is...*

Je voudrais...

Je ______ s'il te plaît.	I would like some bread ______ .
Il ______ s'il vous plaît.	He would like some water ______ .
______ . ______ avoir un café?	Excuse me. May I have a ______ ?
Pardon. ______ m'asseoir?	______ . May I sit down?

Second Go: ..... /..... /.....

Being Polite

Bonjour...au revoir

	hello (on phone)		Have a good trip!
	welcome		Good luck!
	good night		you're welcome
	see you soon		OK
	see you later		what a shame
	see you tomorrow		I'm sorry

Comment ça va?

Hi Sylvie, how are you?

Good evening! I'm fine, and you?

I feel good thank you very much.

May I introduce Marc?

Pleased to meet you.

	How are you? (form.)		Super!
	OK		not bad
	I'm not well.		And you? (form.)
	I don't know.		This is...

Je voudrais...

	I would like some bread please.
	He would like some water please.
	Excuse me. May I have a coffee?
	Excuse me. May I sit down?

Opinions

First Go: ..... /..... /.....

Je pense...

je ______ que...	I think that...	je m' ______ ...	I am interested in...
je ______ que...	I find that...	je ______ ...	I don't like...
je ______ que...	I believe that...	je déteste...	______
j'adore...	______	______ ...	personally...
j' ______ ...	I like...	selon moi...	______

Ça ne m'intéresse pas.
It .... me.

Ça ....
It means nothing to me.

Ça m'a beaucoup ....
I .... liked it.

Ça m'a fait ....
It .... cry.

Es-tu d'accord?

Es-tu d'accord .... ?
.... with me?

Es-tu d'accord .... ?
.... with that?

______	absolutely	______	it depends
bien entendu	______	______	me neither
bien sûr	______	ça m'est égal	______

Les adjectifs

______	friendly
barbant(e)	______
______ / ______	handsome / beautiful
______	good
doué(e)	______
______	fantastic
génial(e)	______
______	bad
sympa / sympathique	______

Use 'parce que' and 'car' to say '.......................'.

Je .... car il est ennuyeux.
I don't like him .... he's ....

Second Go: ..... /..... /.....

Opinions

Je pense...

I think that...	I am interested in...
I find that...	I don't like...
I believe that...	I hate...
I love...	personally...
I like...	in my opinion...

It doesn't interest me.

It means nothing to me.

I really liked it.

It made me cry.

Es-tu d'accord?

Do you agree with me?

Do you agree with that?

absolutely	it depends
of course	me neither
of course	I don't care

Les adjectifs

friendly

boring

handsome / beautiful

good

talented

fantastic

brilliant

bad

nice

Use '..................................' and '..........' to say 'because'.

I don't like him because he's boring.

Opinions

First Go: ..... / ..... / .....

Talking about books, films, music...

Use 'ce' for ______ nouns, 'cette' for ______ nouns, 'cet' for ______ nouns beginning with a ______ and 'ces' for ______ nouns.

______	*this film*	______	*this team*
ces livres *(m)*	______	cet acteur	______
______	*this programme*	cette actrice	______
ces chansons *(f)*	______	______	*this singer (male)*
______	*this band*	______	*this singer (female)*

Qu'est-ce que tu penses de...?

Qu'est-ce que tu ______ de ce magazine?	What did you think of ______ ?
J' ______ le magazine parce qu'il ______ .	I loved ______ because it was funny.
Comment trouves-tu ______ ?	______ the newspaper?
Il ______ car il est ennuyeux.	I don't like it because it's ______ .
Est-ce que tu trouves ______ sympa?	______ this celebrity is ______ ?
Non, je le trouve ______ ... ...parce qu'il m' ______ . ...parce qu'il est ______ .	No, I ______ awful... ...because he annoys me. ...because he is arrogant.

Quel est .... sur ....?
.... is your opinion of this novel?

À ...., il est formidable parce qu' .... Et toi?
In my opinion, it's .... because it makes me laugh. ....?

Je le trouve .... aussi.
I .... great ....

Second Go: ..... /..... /.....

Opinions

Talking about books, films, music...

Use for masculine nouns, for feminine nouns, for masculine nouns and for plural nouns.

	this film		*this team*
	these books		*this actor*
	this programme		*this actress*
	these songs		*this singer (male)*
	this band		*this singer (female)*

Qu'est-ce que tu penses de...?

	What did you think of this magazine?
	I loved the magazine because it was funny.
	How are you finding the newspaper?
	I don't like it because it's boring.
	Do you think this celebrity is nice?
	No, I find him awful... ...because he annoys me. ...because he is arrogant.

What is your opinion of this novel?

In my opinion, it's great because it makes me laugh. And you?

I find it great as well.

Mixed Practice Quizzes

It's time for some quick quizzes to test you on p.3-14. This content crops up time and time again in exams, so don't be tempted to skip past these pages.

Quiz 1

Date: ...... / ...... / ......

1) Translate into English: 'Ça ne me dit rien.'
2) What is the French infinitive for the verb 'to think'?
3) How would you say that you do something 'on Thursdays' in French?
4) Answer this question in French:
   'Quelle est la date de ton anniversaire?'
5) Translate into French: 'I like her because she is talented.'
6) Count from one to twenty in French.
7) Give the formal and informal ways of saying 'please' in French.
8) Which form of 'ce' should you use for a feminine singular noun?
9) How is someone feeling if they say they are 'pas mal'?
10) Translate into English: 'Qu'est-ce que c'est?'

Total:

Quiz 2

Date: ...... / ...... / ......

1) How do you say 'what a shame' in French?
2) If an event took place 'la semaine dernière', when did it happen?
3) List the seven days of the week in French.
4) Translate into English: 'Est-ce que tu trouves ce livre ennuyeux?'
5) In French, give three possible answers to this question:
   'Es-tu d'accord avec moi?'
6) What is 'une dizaine' in English?
7) Give five different question words in French.
8) What is the French word for 'friendly'?
9) Translate into English: 'Il est huit heures moins le quart.'
10) How do you say 'in my opinion' in French?

Total:

Mixed Practice Quizzes

Quiz 3

Date: ...... / ...... / ......

1) Give two ways of saying 'excuse me' in French.
2) What is 325 in French?
3) Translate into English: 'Ça ne va pas bien.'
4) How would you say 'he annoys me' in French?
5) Give the French for 'first', 'third', 'sixth' and 'tenth'.
6) How should 'quel' change to agree with a masculine plural noun?
7) Translate into English: 'Il y avait une vingtaine de croissants.'
8) List the twelve months of the year in French.
9) Translate into French: 'I love the actor because he is nice.'
10) What does 'à tout à l'heure' mean in English?

Total:

Quiz 4

Date: ...... / ...... / ......

1) Translate into French: 'It made me cry.'
2) How do you say '7:20 in the evening' in French?
3) Give three ways you could turn a statement into a question in French.
4) What does 'ça m'est égal' mean in English?
5) Translate into English: 'Je suis désolé — je ne sais pas.'
6) Give an answer to this question in French: 'C'est quel jour?'
7) What does 'neuvième' mean in English?
8) In French, write out 2004 in words.
9) List four positive adjectives you could use to describe someone in French.
10) Answer this question in French: 'Quelle heure est-il?'

Total:

About Yourself and Your Family

First Go: ..... /..... /.....

Je m'appelle...

Je .... Sara et j'ai quinze ans. Je .... le cinq juin.
I'm called Sara and .... I was born on fifth June.

Je suis .... mais je suis ....
I'm British but I'm of Indian origin.

.... est Xavier et mon nom est Deveaux. ...., c'est le quatre mars.
My first name is Xavier and my surname is Deveaux.
My birthday ....

Je .... à Lyon mais j' .... Paris.
I was born in Lyon but I live near Paris.

Parle-moi de ta famille

le père		le beau-père	
	mother		*step-mother*
	brother	le demi-frère	
la sœur		la demi-sœur	
	grandfather		*twin brother*
	grandmother		*twin sister*
	nephew	le mari	
	niece		*wife*

______, il y a neuf personnes.	In my family, there are nine ______.
Je ______ d'une petite famille... ...car ma mère est ______.	I belong to a small family... ...because my mum is an only child.
J'ai un frère qui est ______... ...et un autre qui est ______.	I have one brother who is older than me... ...and ______ who is younger.
Le ______ de mon père ______ d'Italie... ...donc j'ai de la famille ______.	My father's partner comes ______... ...so I have family abroad.

Second Go: ...../...../.....

About Yourself and Your Family

Je m'appelle...

I'm called Sara and I'm fifteen years old. I was born on fifth June.

I'm British but I'm of Indian origin.

My first name is Xavier and my surname is Deveaux.
My birthday is fourth March.

I was born in Lyon but I live near Paris.

Parle-moi de ta famille

	father		***step-father***
	mother		***step-mother***
	brother		***half-brother***
	sister		***half-sister***
	grandfather		***twin brother***
	grandmother		***twin sister***
	nephew		***husband***
	niece		***wife***

	In my family, there are nine people.
	I belong to a small family... ...because my mum is an only child.
	I have one brother who is older than me... ...and another who is younger.
	My father's partner comes from Italy... ...so I have family abroad.

Describing People

First Go: ..... /..... /.....

On décrit les autres

joli(e)	______	______	***hair***
______ / belle	***handsome /*** ______	______	***long***
laid(e)	______	______	***medium-length***
______	***tall***	courts	______
______	***short / small***	ondulés	______
de taille moyenne	______	bouclés / ______	***curly***
clair(e)	______	______	***straight***
______	***dark***		

Elle est comment?

Elle est ______ et jolie.
She is quite tall and pretty.

grosse ______
______ *slim*

'Marron' and 'noisette' .... agree with the noun they're describing.

Elle a les yeux ______.
She has brown eyes.

______ *hazel*
______ *blue*
verts ______

Elle ______ des lunettes.
She wears ______.

______ *jewellery*

Elle a ______ bruns.
She has brown hair.

roux ______
______ *blonde*

Elle a ______ de beauté sur ______.
She has a beauty spot on her face.

une cicatrice ______
beaucoup de ______ *lots of spots*
______ *a beard*

Second Go:
..... /..... /.....

Describing People

On décrit les autres

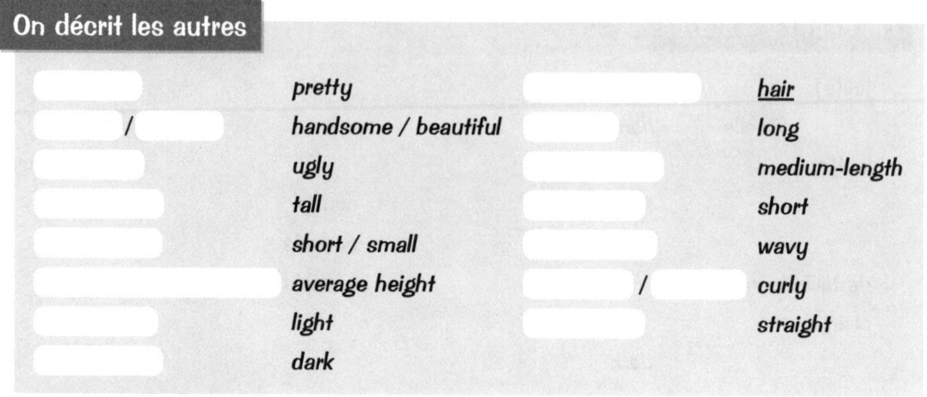

Elle est comment?

She is quite tall and pretty.

fat
slim

' .... ' and ' .... ' .... agree with the noun they're describing.

She has brown eyes.

hazel
blue
green

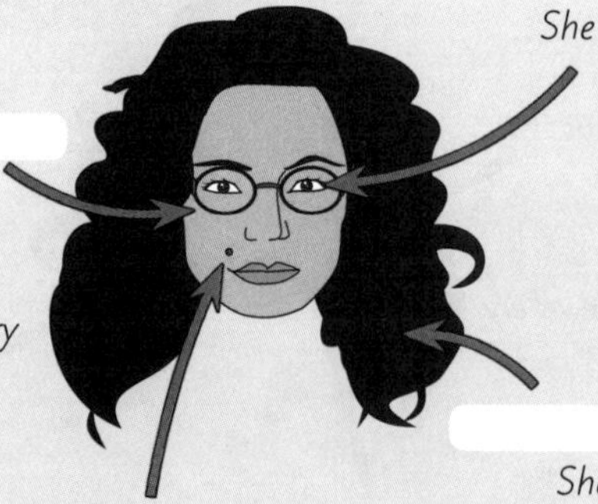

She wears glasses.

jewellery

She has brown hair.

ginger
blonde

She has a beauty spot on her face.

a scar
lots of spots
a beard

Personalities

First Go: ..... /..... /.....

Ma personnalité

Tu as quel genre de caractère?	What .... do you have?
Je suis .... et bavard.	I'm quite lively and ....
Mes amis ....… …je suis vraiment ....… …mais je .... je suis parfois égoïste.	My friends tell me that… …I'm really generous… …but I know that I'm sometimes ....
J'essaie d'être gentil et	I try to be .... and understanding.

Parler des autres

Ma ...., Ann, est vraiment .... et elle est toujours là pour moi quand j'ai un problème.
My best friend, Ann, is really kind and she is always .... when I have a problem.

Watch out for false friends:
'sensible' = '..........'
'le caractère' = '..........'.

Mon frère est .... et il .... aux autres. Pourtant, je suis très fier de ma famille.
My brother is rude and he never thinks about others. ...., I'm .... of my family.

Normalement, ma cousine est très aimable, mais elle est quelquefois .... des autres.
Normally, my cousin is ...., but she is sometimes a bit jealous of others.

Mon meilleur .... s'appelle Loïc. Il est ...., intelligent et ....
My best friend is called Loïc. He's sporty, intelligent and always happy.

Ma petite amie est un peu ...., mais elle est sensible et elle veut toujours ....
My .... is a bit silly, but she is .... and she always wants to help people.

Second Go:
...../...../.....

Personalities

Ma personnalité

	What kind of personality do you have?
	I'm quite lively and talkative.
	My friends tell me that... ...I'm really generous... ...but I know that I'm sometimes selfish.
	I try to be nice and understanding.

Parler des autres

Watch out for false friends:
'..............................' = 'sensitive'
'..............................' = 'personality'.

My best friend, Ann, is really kind and she is always there for me when I have a problem.

My brother is rude and he never thinks about others. However, I'm very proud of my family.

Normally, my cousin is very kind, but she is sometimes a bit jealous of others.

My best friend is called Loïc. He's sporty, intelligent and always happy.

My girlfriend is a bit silly, but she is sensitive and she always wants to help people.

Relationships

First Go: ..... /..... /.....

Se faire des amis

Je connais .... au collège et je me suis fait des amis dans ma ville aussi.
I know lots of people at school and .... in my town as well.

Jacques s'est fait facilement des amis ....
Jacques easily made friends at the youth club.

Je .... nerveux quand je fais de nouvelles connaissances.
I feel nervous when I meet ....

S'entendre bien

Tu ______ avec ta famille?	Do you get on well with your family?
Je ______ bien avec mes parents.	I get on well ______ .
J'ai un bon rapport avec ma sœur.	I have ______ with my sister.
Quelquefois ______ avec mon frère... ...parce qu'il est vraiment gâté. ...parce qu'il n'a pas ______ .	Sometimes I argue with my brother... ...because he is ______ . ...because he doesn't have a sense of humour.

Je .... avec mon .... depuis un an, mais parfois il est casse-pieds.
I've been going out with my boyfriend for a year, but sometimes he's a ....

Mon meilleur ami et moi, ... la plupart du temps. ...., il m'énerve quelquefois.
My best friend and I get on well most of the time. Nevertheless, he .... sometimes.

J'ai .... avec mon cousin. Je suis souvent fâché contre lui.
I have a bad relationship with my cousin. I am often .... with him.

Second Go: ..... /..... /.....

Relationships

Se faire des amis

I know lots of people at school and I've made friends in my town as well.

Jacques easily made friends at the youth club.

I feel nervous when I meet new people.

S'entendre bien

	Do you get on well with your family?
	I get on well with my parents.
	I have a good relationship with my sister.
	Sometimes I argue with my brother... ...because he is really spoilt. ...because he doesn't have a sense of humour.

I've been going out with my boyfriend for a year, but sometimes he's a pain in the neck.

My best friend and I get on well most of the time. Nevertheless, he annoys me sometimes.

I have a bad relationship with my cousin. I am often angry with him.

Partnership

First Go: ..... /..... /.....

Les relations

... ...se sont mariés il y a vingt ans. ...sont ________ .	My parents... ... ________ twenty years ago. ...are divorced.
Mes grands-parents ________ et... ... ________ ensemble. ...se sont tous les deux ________ .	My grandparents are separated and... ...don't live together anymore. ...have ________ remarried.
Mon ________ avait une partenaire,... ...mais maintenant il est célibataire.	My elder brother had a partner,... ...but now he's ________ .
Ma cousine a ________ annoncé ses fiançailles.	My cousin has recently announced ________ .

Pour le mariage

Le mariage montre au monde ....
Marriage .... the world that you love each other.

Pour moi, le mariage est vraiment ....
Je crois qu'il donne .... à la vie de famille.
For me, marriage is really important.
I believe that it gives structure to ....

......................., je voudrais me marier et avoir ....
In the future, I'd like to .... and have children.

Contre le mariage

De nos jours, le mariage .... devenir ....
......................., marriage is starting to become old-fashioned.

.... sont trop .... Avec l'argent, je préférerais acheter une maison.
Weddings are too expensive. With the money, ... to buy a house.

Pour moi, ce qui est .... c'est l'amour et ....
On peut être avec quelqu'un et avoir des enfants sans l'épouser.
..................., what's more important is .... and trust. You can be with someone and have children without ....

Second Go: ...../...../.....	# Partnership

Les relations

	My parents... ...got married twenty years ago. ...are divorced.
	My grandparents are separated and... ...don't live together anymore. ...have both remarried.
	My elder brother had a partner,... ...but now he's single.
	My cousin has recently announced her engagement.

Pour le mariage

Marriage shows the world that you love each other.

For me, marriage is really important. I believe that it gives structure to family life.

In the future, I'd like to get married and have children.

Contre le mariage

These days, marriage is starting to become old-fashioned.

Weddings are too expensive. With the money, I would prefer to buy a house.

For me, what's more important is love and trust. You can be with someone and have children without marrying them.

Mixed Practice Quizzes

Ready for another round of quizzes? These ones test the content on p.17-26. Give the questions a go, then mark your answers to see how you've got on.

Quiz 1

Date: ...... / ...... / ......

1) True or false? The French for 'I was born' is 'j'ai né'.
2) How do you say 'very kind' in French?
3) Translate into French: 'I feel nervous when I meet new people.'
4) Give two verbs that mean 'to marry' in French.
5) Translate into English: 'Elle a les cheveux roux et elle porte des lunettes.'
6) What is 'un beau-père' in English?
7) In French, give one reason why someone might want to get married.
8) How do you say 'a bit jealous' in French?
9) Translate into English: 'Je sais que je suis assez bavard.'
10) Give three ways of describing the length of someone's hair in French.

Total:

Quiz 2

Date: ...... / ...... / ......

1) Translate into English: 'Ma jumelle est toujours là pour moi.'
2) What does this sentence mean in English?
   'J'habite à Manchester mais je suis née en Écosse.'
3) Translate into English: 'Normalement, je m'entends bien avec mon oncle.'
4) What does 'montre au monde' mean in English?
5) Answer this question with a sentence in French:
   'Tu as quel genre de caractère?'
6) Translate into French: 'He has a scar on his face.'
7) What does the phrase 'vraiment vif' mean in English?
8) Give the French infinitive for the verb 'to argue'.
9) Translate into English:
   'Je fais partie d'une grande famille car j'ai plusieurs frères et sœurs.'
10) In French, give a full sentence to say how many people are in your family.

Total:

Mixed Practice Quizzes

Quiz 3

Date: ...... / ...... / ......

1) Translate into French: 'My half-brother never thinks about others.'
2) Give an answer to this question in French:
'Tu t'entends bien avec ta famille?'
3) Translate into French: 'My parents don't live together anymore.'
4) What does 'de nos jours' mean in English?
5) How do you say 'he's a pain in the neck' in French?
6) Translate into English: 'Ma mère n'a ni frères ni sœurs.'
7) What's special about the adjectives 'marron' and 'noisette'?
8) How do you say 'trust is important' in French?
9) What does this sentence mean in English?
'Mon amie a les yeux bleus et elle est très jolie, intelligente et heureuse.'
10) Translate into French: 'My elder brother is single.'

Total:

Quiz 4

Date: ...... / ...... / ......

1) In French, give one reason why someone might be opposed to marriage.
2) Translate into French: 'Sometimes I argue with my father.'
3) True or false? 'Les cheveux raides' means 'curly hair'.
4) What does 'se faire des amis' mean in English?
5) Translate into English: 'Ma sœur a récemment annoncé ses fiançailles.'
6) Give the French for 'light' and 'dark'.
7) Translate into French: 'My friends tell me that I'm a bit selfish.'
8) What does this sentence mean in English?
'Elle veut toujours aider les autres.'
9) Give two French adjectives you can use to describe someone's height.
10) Translate into French: 'I am often angry with him.'

Total:

Music

First Go: ..... /..... /.....

La musique

'jouer ....' = to play a musical instrument

Est-ce que tu _____ instrument de musique?	Do you play a _____?
Je _____ dans un orchestre... **...et j'apprends à jouer de la batterie.**	I play the violin in an _____... ...and I'm learning to play the _____.
La musicienne joue de la guitare... **...et chante _____.**	The _____ plays the guitar... ...and sings at her concerts.
Je fais partie d'un groupe... **...et _____ tous les samedis.**	_____ a band... ...and we rehearse every Saturday.
Quand _____ petit... **...je chantais dans une chorale.**	When I was younger... ...I used to sing in a _____.

Quel genre préfères-tu?

La .... est mon genre de musique préféré. Je verrai bientôt mon .... en concert.
Pop music is my favourite music genre. I will see my favourite singer .... soon.

Mon grand-père préfère la musique rock .... musique ....
My grandad prefers .... to classical music.

Ma sœur détestait écouter .... quand elle avait mon âge mais elle .... la danse.
My sister hated listening to rap when .... but she liked .... a lot.

J'aime autant regarder .... qu'écouter des ....
I like watching music videos as much as listening to songs.

À mon avis, ... sont quelquefois trop ....
In my opinion, techno songs are .... too weird.

Second Go: ..... /..... /.....	**Music**

La musique

'...............................' = to play a musical instrument

	Do you play a musical instrument?
	I play the violin in an orchestra... ...and I'm learning to play the drums.
	The musician plays the guitar... ...and sings at her concerts.
	I am part of a band... ...and we rehearse every Saturday.
	When I was younger... ...I used to sing in a choir.

Quel genre préfères-tu?

Pop music is my favourite music genre. I will see my favourite singer in concert soon.

My grandad prefers rock music to classical music.

My sister hated listening to rap when she was my age but she liked dance music a lot.

I like watching music videos as much as listening to songs.

In my opinion, techno songs are sometimes too weird.

Cinema

First Go: ..... /..... /.....

Regardons un film

l'intrigue (f)			*exciting*
	story	ennuyeux / ennuyeuse	
les effets (m)	*special effects*		
	action	doué(e)	
			believable
l'acteur (m)			*famous*
	actress		
	character	entraînant(e)	
		formidable	

Le film était ______ long... ...que je ______ avant la fin.	The film was so long... ...I fell asleep ______.
J'ai ______ oublier tous mes problèmes... ... ______ le film.	I managed to ______ all my problems... ...as I watched the film.

Allons au cinéma

J'aime .... mais je n'aime pas les ....
I like action films but I don't like cartoons.

Genres with an adjective need to .... in the plural, e.g. 'les films comiques', but genres with 'de + ...' don't, e.g. 'les films d'action'.

Les films d'horreur ...., mais j'adore les films d'amour.
.... *scare me, but I love* ....

J'aime aller .... pour voir des films sur grand écran, mais .... m'énervent.
I like going to the cinema to see films ...., *but the trailers annoy me.*

Je trouve que .... sont plus divertissants que les films d'animation.
I find comedies .... *than* ....

Je peux acheter les billets de cinéma .... parce que je suis jeune.
I can buy .... *at a reduced price because I'm* ....

Second Go:
..... / ..... / .....

Cinema

Regardons un film

	plot		exciting
	story	/	boring
	special effects		
	action		talented
	actor		believable
	actress		famous
	character		catchy
			great

	The film was so long... ...I fell asleep before the end.
	I managed to forget all my problems... ...as I watched the film.

Allons au cinéma

Genres with an .... need to .... in the plural, e.g. 'les films ....', but genres with '....................' don't, e.g. 'les films ....'.

I like action films but I don't like cartoons.

Horror films scare me, but I love romantic films.

I like going to the cinema to see films on the big screen, but the trailers annoy me.

I find comedies more entertaining than animated films.

I can buy cinema tickets at a reduced price because I'm young.

TV

First Go:
..... /..... /.....

La télévision

	programme	le jeu	game show
le feuilleton		les séries (f)	crime shows
	reality TV	les séries (f)	period dramas
	the news	à la télé	

J'aime regarder...

Mon .... préféré est regarder la télévision car c'est ....
My favourite hobby is watching television because it's relaxing.

J'aime .... les documentaires.
I like watching ....

Je trouve .... intéressant parce qu'on apprend beaucoup .... on les regarde.
I find this type of programme interesting because you .... *when you watch them.*

Je préfère regarder les chaînes de télé qui ne .... pas de ....
I prefer watching the .... *that don't broadcast adverts.*

Tu regardes beaucoup de télé?

Je regarde ______ la télévision.	I often watch television.
Mes parents ______ que... ...je passe trop de temps devant la télé... ... ______ faire mes devoirs.	My parents think that... ...I spend too much time ______ the TV... ...instead of doing my homework.
J'ai besoin de regarder la télé... ...pour me reposer... ...après une ______ .	______ watch TV... ...in order to ______ ... ...after a day of lessons.

Second Go: ..... /..... /.....

TV

La télévision

programme	game show
soap opera	crime shows
reality TV	period dramas
the news	on TV

J'aime regarder...

My favourite hobby is watching television because it's relaxing.

I like watching documentaries.

I find this type of programme interesting because you learn a lot when you watch them.

I prefer watching the TV channels that don't broadcast adverts.

Tu regardes beaucoup de télé?

	I often watch television.
	My parents think that... ...I spend too much time in front of the TV... ...instead of doing my homework.
	I need to watch TV... ...in order to relax... ...after a day of lessons.

Mixed Practice Quizzes

Those pages were action-packed — now have a go at these practice quizzes. Each quiz tests the content on p.29-34. On your marks... get set... allez!

Quiz 1

Date: ...... / ...... / ......

1) Name three different types of TV programme in French.
2) In French, give a sentence saying what your favourite genre of music is.
3) Translate into French: 'The special effects were great.'
4) What does the verb 'se reposer' mean in English?
5) What does this sentence mean in English?
   'Les dessins animés sont plus divertissants que les feuilletons.'
6) Translate into English: 'Je faisais partie d'une chorale.'
7) What does 'ce genre d'émission' mean in English?
8) Translate into French: 'Horror films scare me.'
9) True or false? 'To play an instrument' is
   'jouer à un instrument' in French.
10) Translate into French: 'I often watch the news.'

Total:

Quiz 2

Date: ...... / ...... / ......

1) How do you say 'on the big screen' in French?
2) In French, give a sentence to say what type of music you dislike.
3) Translate into French: 'My favourite hobby is watching crime shows.'
4) What are 'les bandes-annonces' in English?
5) How do you say 'classical music' in French?
6) True or false? 'Sur la télé' means 'on TV'.
7) What does this sentence mean in English?
   'Ils aiment autant écouter le rap que regarder les clips.'
8) Give the French for three different film genres.
9) Translate into French: 'We rehearse for the concert.'
10) What is the French infinitive of the verb 'to annoy'?

Total:

Mixed Practice Quizzes

Quiz 3

Date: ...... / ...... / ......

1) Translate into French: 'In my opinion, the characters weren't believable.'
2) What does 'quand elle avait mon âge' mean in English?
3) True or false? If someone is 'doué', it means they are famous.
4) Translate into English:
   'Je déteste les chaînes de télé qui diffusent les publicités.'
5) What does 'la musique entraînante' mean in English?
6) Give a sentence in French to say what types of films you enjoy watching and why.
7) Translate into French: 'I like watching TV after a day of lessons.'
8) How do you say 'cinema tickets' in French?
9) What does 'la batterie' mean in English?
10) How do you say 'when I was younger' in French?

Total:

Quiz 4

Date: ...... / ...... / ......

1) Translate into French: 'We will see our favourite band in concert soon.'
2) What does this sentence mean in English?
   'Le film d'amour que j'ai regardé était vraiment ennuyeux.'
3) True or false? 'L'intrigue' means 'plot'.
4) Translate into English:
   'J'ai l'impression que les gens regardent trop de télé.'
5) How do you say 'instead of watching game shows' in French?
6) What does this sentence mean in English?
   'Le musicien joue du violon dans un orchestre.'
7) Translate into English: 'Je me suis endormi avant la fin du film.'
8) What does this sentence mean in English?
   'Ma petite sœur passe beaucoup de temps devant la télé.'
9) Translate into French: 'I'm learning to play the guitar.'
10) What does 'à tarif réduit' mean in English?

Total:

Food

First Go: ..... /..... /.....

Les fruits et les légumes

	apple		cauliflower
	pear	les haricots (m) verts	
la framboise			mushroom
	strawberry	la pomme	potato
	grapes	les pois (m)	peas
l'ananas (m)			

Le goût

épicé(e)	
	sweet
	salty
amer / amère	
bien	well cooked

D'autre nourriture

	bread		butter
	rice	l'œuf (m)	
	pasta	le poulet	
les frites (f)			beef
	milk	le jambon	
le fromage		le thon	

Je mange...

Je préfère manger du .... plutôt que de la viande.
I prefer eating fish rather than ....

.... est .... pour la santé et plus nourrissant.
Fish is better for your .... and more ....

Mon plat préféré est un ....
My .... is a toasted ham and cheese sandwich.

Je préfère la saucisse aux ....
I prefer .... to seafood.

Je ne mange pas de chou parce que .... dégoûtant.
I don't eat .... because I find it ....

J'aime manger .... parce que j'aime le goût.
I like eating lamb because I like ....

Je .... manger moins de nourriture sucrée parce que .... meilleur pour ma santé.
I should eat less .... because that would be better for my health.

Second Go: ..... /..... /.....

Food

Les fruits et les légumes

- apple
- pear
- raspberry
- strawberry
- grapes
- pineapple

- cauliflower
- green beans
- mushroom
- potato
- peas

Le goût

- spicy
- sweet
- salty
- bitter
- well cooked

D'autre nourriture

- bread
- rice
- pasta
- chips
- milk
- cheese

- butter
- egg
- chicken
- beef
- ham
- tuna

Je mange...

I prefer eating fish rather than meat.

Fish is better for your health and more nourishing.

My favourite meal is a toasted ham and cheese sandwich.

I prefer sausage to seafood.

I don't eat cabbage because I find it disgusting.

I like eating lamb because I like the taste.

I should eat less sugary food because that would be better for my health.

Eating Out

First Go: ..... / ..... / .....

Au restaurant

la carte	______	le café	______
______ d'œuvre	*starter*	______	*beer*
le plat ______	*main meal*	le serveur	______
la boisson	______	la serveuse	______
l'eau *(f)* ______	*still water*	______	*the bill*
l'eau *(f)* ______	*fizzy water*	______	*to take away*
______	*tea*	avoir ______ / ______	*to be thirsty / hungry*

Bon appétit!

J'ai ______ des escargots... ...et mon père a commandé du potage et un ______.	I ordered the ______... ...and my father ordered the ______ and a glass of wine.
Comme ______, j'ai mangé des ______ et une glace.	For dessert, I ate pancakes and an ______.
Ce ______ beaucoup de plats ______ et végétaliens.	This restaurant serves lots of vegetarian and ______ dishes.
J'aime manger au ______... ...parce qu'on peut ______... ...qu'on ne ______ jamais chez soi.	______ in restaurants... ...because you can try dishes... ...that you would never cook ______.
Je préfère ______ mexicaine à ______ chinoise.	I prefer Mexican food to Chinese food.
Je suis ______ à l'ail... ...donc c'est difficile de trouver des ______ français... ...______ manger.	I am allergic to garlic... ...so ______ to find French restaurants... ...where I can eat.
Je me suis ______ du saumon... ...parce qu'il ______ froid.	I complained about the ______... ...because it was cold.

Second Go: ..... /..... /.....

Eating Out

Au restaurant

	menu		coffee
	starter		beer
	main meal		waiter
	drink		waitress
	still water		the bill
	fizzy water		to take away
	tea	/	to be thirsty / hungry

Bon appétit!

	I ordered the snails... ...and my father ordered the soup and a glass of wine.
	For dessert, I ate pancakes and an ice cream.
	This restaurant serves lots of vegetarian and vegan dishes.
	I like eating in restaurants... ...because you can try dishes... ...that you would never cook at home.
	I prefer Mexican food to Chinese food.
	I am allergic to garlic... ...so it's hard to find French restaurants... ...where I can eat.
	I complained about the salmon... ...because it was cold.

Sports

First Go: ..... /..... /.....

Les sports

______ / football	*football*	______	*rowing*
______	*badminton*	______	*skiing*
______	*netball*	l'équitation *(f)*	______
la natation	______	______	*athletics*

Faire du sport

1. faire ___ + sport = to do a sport. → .... gymnastique après le collège. *I do gymnastics after school.*

2. jouer ___ + sport = to play a sport. → .... rugby deux fois par semaine. *I play rugby twice a week.*

3. pratiquer ___ / ___ + sport = to practise a sport. → .... voile pendant les vacances. *We practise sailing during the holidays.*

Mon sport préféré

Je préfère ______ aux ______ ... ...parce qu'on joue seulement pour soi-même.	I prefer individual sports to team sports... ...because you play just for ______.
Je suis ______ basket... ...et j'ai regardé un match ______ au stade.	I am a ______ fan... ...and I watched an exciting match ______.
Un match de ______ est plus captivant qu'une ______ ... ...parce qu'on peut voir les expressions des joueurs.	A tennis match is more ______ than a car race... ...because you can see the ______ expressions.
Faire du vélo ______ ... ...mais je fais des randonnées.	______ doesn't interest me... ...but I ______.

Second Go:
..... /..... /.....

Sports

Les sports

/	football		rowing
	badminton		skiing
	netball		horse riding
	swimming		athletics

Faire du sport

1. + sport = to do a sport. → *I do gymnastics after school.*

2. + sport = to play a sport. → *I play rugby twice a week.*

3. + sport = to practise a sport. → *We practise sailing during the holidays.*

Mon sport préféré

	I prefer individual sports to team sports... ...because you play just for yourself.
	I am a basketball fan... ...and I watched an exciting match at the stadium.
	A tennis match is more engaging than a car race... ...because you can see the players' expressions.
	Cycling doesn't interest me... ...but I go on walks.

Sports

First Go: ..... /..... /.....

Je suis sportif

J' ________ faire du sport... ... ________ vendredi. ...le ________ .	I try to do sport... ...every Friday. ...at the weekend.
J'aime ________ avec d'autres personnes... ...donc je fais du ________ .	I like training with other people... ...so I do hockey.
Je vais au ________ ... ...qui a un terrain de sport et une ________ .	I go to the sports centre... ...which has a ________ and a pool.
Quelquefois c'est difficile de ________ ... ...particulièrement quand je suis ________ ________ , ce qui est souvent le cas.	________ it's difficult to motivate myself... ...especially when I'm already tired, which is ________ .
Nous ________ les matchs au stade, ce que je n'aime pas... ...parce qu'ils me rendent nerveux. ...car ils sont trop ________ .	We play matches at the ________ , which I don't like... ...because they ________ . ...because they are too competitive.

Le tournoi

Mon .... a joué un match la semaine dernière.
My football team played a match ....

Nous .... le match mais j'ai marqué un but.
We lost the match but I ....

Je n'avais pas fait assez .... pour le tournoi.
I hadn't done enough training for the ....

Il va gagner .... s'il continue à ....!
He's going .... the race if he continues to run fast!

Il ne faut pas .... pendant le jeu.
You mustn't cheat .... the game.

Second Go: ..... /..... /.....

Sports

Je suis sportif

	I try to do sport... ...every Friday. ...at the weekend.
	I like training with other people... ...so I do hockey.
	I go to the sports centre... ...which has a sports field and a pool.
	Sometimes it's difficult to motivate myself... ...especially when I'm already tired, which is often the case.
	We play matches at the stadium, which I don't like... ...because they make me nervous. ...because they are too competitive.

Le tournoi

My football team played a match last week.

We lost the match but I scored a goal.

I hadn't done enough training for the tournament.

You mustn't cheat during the game.

He's going to win the race if he continues to run fast!

Mixed Practice Quizzes

You've made it to the end of this topic — phew. These quizzes test the content on p.37-44. Have a go at the questions and give yourself a mark out of ten.

Quiz 1

Date: ...... / ...... / ......

1) Give the French for 'starter', 'main meal' and 'dessert'.
2) How do you say 'I like the taste' in French?
3) Translate into French: 'We practise horse riding at the weekend.'
4) How do you say 'a football team' in French?
5) What does 'ce qui est souvent le cas' mean in English?
6) What does this mean in English?
   'Je préfère la cuisine mexicaine à la cuisine italienne.'
7) Translate into English: 'Les tournois me rendent nerveux.'
8) How would you say 'I am allergic to seafood' in French?
9) True or false? 'Faire des randonnées' means 'to go on walks'.
10) Translate into English: 'Je devrais manger plus de légumes.'

Total:

Quiz 2

Date: ...... / ...... / ......

1) Translate into French: 'My team won the match and I scored a goal.'
2) Translate into English:
   'Manger moins de nourriture salée serait meilleur pour ma santé.'
3) Translate into French: 'I prefer team sports to individual sports.'
4) In a café, when would you use the French verb 'commander'?
5) What does this mean in English?
   'Nous n'avons pas fait assez d'entraînement.'
6) What is 'un terrain de sport' in English?
7) How do you say that you're hungry and thirsty in French?
8) Name three different fruits in French.
9) Give the missing word to complete this sentence and then translate it into English: 'Je fais ... vélo après le collège.'
10) What does the verb 'tricher' mean in English?

Total:

Mixed Practice Quizzes

Quiz 3

Date: ...... / ...... / ......

1) Give the French for four different sports.
2) Translate into English: 'Je préfère manger de la viande plutôt que du poisson.'
3) Translate into French: 'I really want to win the hockey match.'
4) What does this sentence mean in English? 'Le match de tennis était très captivant.'
5) How do you say 'the bill' in French?
6) Translate into French: 'I try to do sport every Sunday.'
7) Give the names of two different dairy products in French.
8) Translate into French: 'Athletics doesn't interest me.'
9) What does the verb 'emporter' mean in English?
10) True or false? 'To train' in French is 'se traîner'.

Total:

Quiz 4

Date: ...... / ...... / ......

1) What does this mean in English? 'Le thon est nourrissant.'
2) Translate into English: 'C'est difficile de trouver des restaurants où je peux manger.'
3) How do you say 'I am a fan of swimming' in French?
4) What does 'goûter les plats' mean in English?
5) Give three French adjectives to describe the taste of food.
6) Give the missing word to complete this sentence and then translate it into English: 'Je joue ... netball tous les samedis.'
7) How do you say 'I go to the sports centre' in French?
8) Translate into French: 'This restaurant serves lots of vegetarian dishes.'
9) Give the French for three different vegetables.
10) Translate into English: 'Je me suis plaint du poulet.'

Total:

Technology

First Go: ...../...../.....

La technologie

J'utilise ______ tous les jours... ...et je trouve l' ______ utile.	I use my tablet ______ ... ...and I find the touch screen ______ .
Mon ______ portable est idéal... ...pour naviguer sur Internet et lire mon ______ électronique.	My laptop is ideal... ...for ______ the Internet and for reading my email.
J' ______ et je ______ des dizaines de textos par jour.	I send and receive dozens of ______ per day.
Les textos ______ la conversation.	______ have replaced conversation.
Je ne pourrais pas vivre sans mon ______ .	I ______ without my mobile phone.
Mes parents peuvent ______ pour savoir où je suis... ...et vérifier que je suis ______ .	My parents can phone me to find out where I am... ...and ______ I'm safe.

Internet

Je .... en ligne parce que c'est plus pratique.
I shop online because it's ....

Je fais des recherches sur Internet car .... sont très utiles.
I .... on the Internet because factual websites are very ....

Je peux jouer à des jeux en ligne avec mes copains .... de ma chambre.
I can play .... with my friends without leaving my bedroom.

Je préfère télécharger les albums .... d'acheter un CD.
I prefer .... albums instead of buying a CD.

On doit être .... en ligne et penser à ce qu'on écrit.
You need to be careful online and .... what you write.

Il faut protéger ses .... et ne pas cliquer sur les liens suspects.
You must protect your passwords and not click on .... links.

Second Go: ..... /..... /.....	

Technology

La technologie

	I use my tablet every day... ...and I find the touch screen useful.
	My laptop is ideal... ...for browsing the Internet and for reading my email.
	I send and receive dozens of text messages per day.
	Text messages have replaced conversation.
	I couldn't live without my mobile phone.
	My parents can phone me to find out where I am... ...and check I'm safe.

Internet

I shop online because it's more practical.

I do research on the Internet because factual websites are very useful.

I can play online games with my friends without leaving my bedroom.

I prefer downloading albums instead of buying a CD.

You need to be careful online and think about what you write.

You must protect your passwords and not click on suspicious links.

Social Media

First Go: ..... /..... /.....

Les avantages

Les .... me permettent d'être à jour avec des .... importantes.
Social media sites allow me to .... with important news.

Ils rendent l'organisation des .... sociaux facile.
.... *organising social events easy.*

Je peux mettre les photos de mes vacances en ligne pour les .... mes amis.
I can .... photos of my holidays to show my friends.

Je peux .... mes articles de blog et tchatter avec mes amis.
I can share my .... and .... with my friends.

Ils .... de rencontrer ceux qui .... les mêmes intérêts que moi.
It allows me to .... those who share the same interests as me.

.... réseaux sociaux, c'est facile de rester en contact avec ma famille.
Thanks to social networks, it's easy to .... with my family.

Les inconvénients

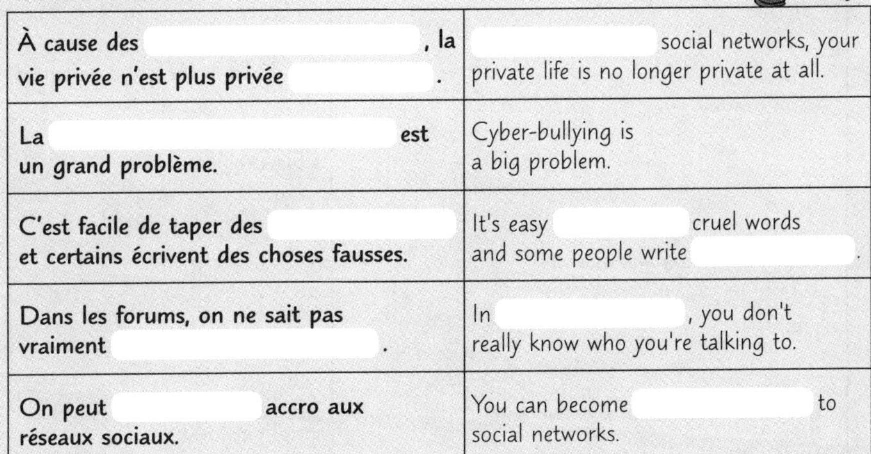

À cause des ...., la vie privée n'est plus privée	.... social networks, your private life is no longer private at all.
La .... est un grand problème.	Cyber-bullying is a big problem.
C'est facile de taper des .... et certains écrivent des choses fausses.	It's easy .... cruel words and some people write ....
Dans les forums, on ne sait pas vraiment	In ...., you don't really know who you're talking to.
On peut .... accro aux réseaux sociaux.	You can become .... to social networks.

Second Go: ...../...../.....

Social Media

Les avantages

Social media sites allow me to keep up to date with important news.

It makes organising social events easy.

I can upload photos of my holidays to show my friends.

I can share my blog articles and chat online with my friends.

It allows me to meet those who share the same interests as me.

Thanks to social networks, it's easy to stay in contact with my family.

Les inconvénients

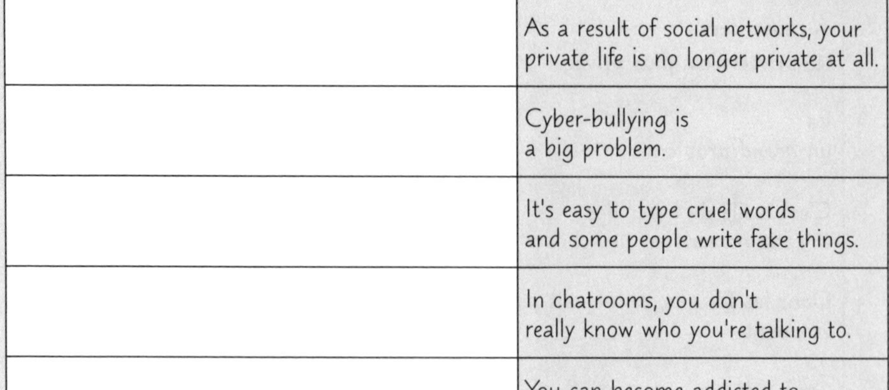

	As a result of social networks, your private life is no longer private at all.
	Cyber-bullying is a big problem.
	It's easy to type cruel words and some people write fake things.
	In chatrooms, you don't really know who you're talking to.
	You can become addicted to social networks.

Mixed Practice Quizzes

There are quite a few tricky phrases and words on p.47-50. Make sure you've got to grips with them by having a go at each of these mixed practice quizzes.

Quiz 1

Date: ...... / ...... / ......

1) What does 'télécharger' mean in English?
2) True or false? 'Rencontrer' means 'to show'.
3) In French, give an example of something you can do online.
4) Translate into English:
   'Dans les forums, certaines personnes tapent les mots cruels.'
5) Translate into French: 'You need to be careful.'
6) What does 'penser à ce qu'on écrit' mean in English?
7) Give the French for 'cyber-bullying'.
8) Translate into French: 'I find my mobile phone very useful.'
9) Give the French for 'passwords'.
10) How do you say 'social events' in French?

Total:

Quiz 2

Date: ...... / ...... / ......

1) True or false? 'En sécurité' means 'safe'.
2) How do you say 'thanks to social networks' in French?
3) In French, give one advantage of social media.
4) True or false? 'Remplacer' means 'to send'.
5) What does 'à cause de' mean in English?
6) Give the French for 'touch screen'.
7) What does this sentence mean in English?
   'Je peux rencontrer ceux qui partagent les mêmes intérêts que moi.'
8) Give the French for 'to upload'.
9) Translate into English:
   'J'utilise ma tablette pour lire mon courrier électronique.'
10) How do you say 'to stay in contact' in French?

Total:

Mixed Practice Quizzes

Quiz 3

Date: ...... / ...... / ......

1) How do you say 'important news' in French?
2) Translate into French: 'I play online games with my cousins.'
3) Give the French for 'blog articles'.
4) In French, give one benefit of using mobile phones.
5) Give the French for 'to do research online'.
6) What does this sentence mean in English?
   'Certains écrivent des choses fausses.'
7) True or false? 'Être à jour' means 'to keep up to date'.
8) Translate into French: 'My parents can phone me.'
9) Give the French for 'every day'.
10) Translate into English: 'On peut devenir accro aux sites sociaux.'

Total:

Quiz 4

Date: ...... / ...... / ......

1) What is the French infinitive of the verb 'to protect'?
2) Translate into French: 'Factual websites make research really easy.'
3) What does this sentence mean in English?
   'Ne cliquez pas sur les liens suspects.'
4) How do you say 'to browse the Internet' in French?
5) In French, give one disadvantage of social media.
6) Give the French for 'laptop'.
7) How do you say 'to chat with my friends' in French?
8) Translate into English: 'Je ne pourrais pas vivre sans mon portable.'
9) What is 'to shop online' in French?
10) What does this sentence mean in English?
   'Mes amis et moi envoyons et recevons beaucoup de textos.'

Total:

Festivals in French-Speaking Countries

First Go: ...../...../.....

Les fêtes

la fête du travail	....	....	*New Year's Day*
....	*Mother's / Father's Day*	....	*Happy New Year!*
.... /		....	*Happy birthday!*
....	*Valentine's Day*	Félicitations!	....
la fête	*Epiphany / Twelfth Night*	Bonne chance!	....

J'aime les .... parce que les écoles et les .... sont	I like bank holidays because .... and offices are closed.
.... fêtes sont... ...trop ....trop ....très impressionnantes.	Some festivals are... ...too commercial. ...too sentimental. ...very ....
On fait des	People do traditional dances.
La Saint-Sylvestre, on la fête ....avec .... et ses copains. ...et on prend	On ...., people .... at midnight... ...with family and ....and make resolutions.

La fête nationale

Le quatorze juillet est le jour de la ....
The .... is Bastille Day.

La fête nationale est un .... qu'on célèbre en France.
Bastille Day is an historical event that people .... in France.

Il y a .... pour la célébrer, comme un défilé militaire à Paris.
There are many events to .... it, like a military .... in Paris.

Beaucoup de gens .... aux couleurs ....
.... dress in the colours of the French flag.

J'aime regarder les feux d'artifice parce qu'ils sont ....
I like watching the .... because they're always amazing.

Second Go: ..... /..... /.....

Festivals in French-Speaking Countries

Les fêtes

	May Day
	Mother's / Father's Day
	Valentine's Day
	Epiphany / Twelfth Night
	New Year's Day
	Happy New Year!
	Happy birthday!
	Congratulations!
	Good luck!

	I like bank holidays because schools and offices are closed.
	Some festivals are... ...too commercial. ...too sentimental. ...very impressive.
	People do traditional dances.
	On New Year's Eve, people celebrate at midnight... ...with family and friends. ...and make resolutions.

La fête nationale

The fourteenth of July is Bastille Day.

Bastille Day is an historical event that people celebrate in France.

There are many events to celebrate it, like a military procession in Paris.

Lots of people dress in the colours of the French flag.

I like watching the fireworks because they're always amazing.

Festivals in French-Speaking Countries

First Go: ..... / ..... / .....

La fête des rois

Le six janvier, toute la ______ ... ...se retrouve pour ______ .	On sixth January, all the extended family... ... ______ for Twelfth Night.
Dans ______ ______ de la France... ...on mange une 'galette des rois'... ...qui est un type de ______ .	In a large part of France... ... ______ a 'galette des rois'... ...which is a type of round cake.
Dans le sud ______ ,... ...on ______ un 'gâteau des rois',... ...une brioche en forme de couronne.	______ of France,... ...people make a 'gâteau des rois',... ...a brioche ______ ______ .
On ______ une fève dans la galette.	A ______ is hidden in the cake.
La personne qui trouve la fève devient ______ .	The person who ______ becomes the king or queen.
Il ou elle ______ une couronne.	He or she wears a ______ .

Poisson d'avril!

Le premier avril, on .... aux autres.
On ...., people play tricks ....

On met des poissons en papier sur .... de ses amis.
People put .... on their friends' backs.

On .... «poisson d'avril!» quand l'ami s'en rend compte.
People shout 'poisson d'avril!' when their friend ....

...................................., mon ami m'a raconté une plaisanterie et ....
Last year, my friend .... and played a trick on me.

Second Go: ..... /..... /.....

Festivals in French-Speaking Countries

La fête des rois

	On sixth January, all the extended family... ...meet for Twelfth Night.
	In a large part of France... ...people eat a 'galette des rois'... ...which is a type of round cake.
	In the south of France,... ...people make a 'gâteau des rois',... ...a brioche in the shape of a crown.
	A charm is hidden in the cake.
	The person who finds the charm becomes the king or queen.
	He or she wears a crown.

Poisson d'avril!

On first April, people play tricks on others.

People put paper fish on their friends' backs.

People shout 'poisson d'avril!' when their friend realises.

Last year, my friend told me a joke and played a trick on me.

Religious Festivals and Customs

First Go: ..... /..... /.....

La foi

______ / ______	*religious*	______	*synagogue*
juif / juive	______	______	*mosque*
______	*Muslim*	l'église *(f)*	______
______	*Christian*	______	*Easter*
athée	______	le carême	______

Joyeux Noël!

Nous .... des cadeaux sous le sapin de Noël.
We put .... under the ....

Nous les ouvrons soit après .... soit le jour de Noël.
We .... either after midnight mass or on ....

'Le réveillon' est .... après minuit la veille de Noël.
'Le réveillon' is the dinner we eat after midnight ....

Nous mangeons de l'oie ou .... pour le réveillon.
We eat .... or turkey for 'le réveillon'.

.............................., ma grand-mère fait une bûche de Noël.
Each year, my grandmother makes a ....

La Hanoukka

La Hanoukka est une fête juive. On .... et on prie ensemble.
.... is a Jewish festival. People light candles and ....

On la fête pendant huit jours et on .... des cadeaux.
People celebrate it .... and they exchange ....

L'Aïd al-Fitr

L'Aïd al-Fitr .... du mois du ramadan. Pour la fêter, on mange un .... avec sa famille.
.... marks the end of the month of Ramadan. ...., people eat a large meal with their family.

Au cours du ramadan, ... ne .... ni manger ni boire de l'aube au coucher du soleil.
During Ramadan, Muslims should neither eat nor drink from ....

Second Go: ...../...../.....

Religious Festivals and Customs

La foi

/	religious		synagogue
/	Jewish		mosque
	Muslim		church
	Christian		Easter
	atheist		Lent

Joyeux Noël!

We put presents under the Christmas tree.

We open them either after midnight mass or on Christmas Day.

'Le réveillon' is the dinner we eat after midnight on Christmas Eve.

We eat goose or turkey for 'le réveillon'.

Each year, my grandmother makes a yule log.

La Hanoukka

Hanukkah is a Jewish festival. People light candles and pray together.

People celebrate it for eight days and they exchange gifts.

L'Aïd al-Fitr

Eid al-Fitr marks the end of the month of Ramadan. To celebrate it, people eat a large meal with their family.

During Ramadan, Muslims should neither eat nor drink from dawn until sunset.

Mixed Practice Quizzes

You can celebrate coming to the end of this topic with a round of festive quizzes — after all, practice makes perfect. These tests cover the content on p.53-58.

Quiz 1

Date: ...... / ...... / ......

1) Give the name for three different festivals in French.
2) What does the verb 'se retrouver' mean in English?
3) Translate into French: 'People light candles to celebrate Hanukkah.'
4) What do they call 'Twelfth Night' in French?
5) Translate into English: 'Nous nous habillons aux couleurs tricolores.'
6) Give the French for 'Lent'.
7) Answer this question with a sentence in French: 'Qu'est-ce qu'une galette des rois?'
8) Translate into English: 'J'ai joué un tour à mon meilleur ami.'
9) Translate into French: 'Schools and offices are closed.'
10) True or false? The French for 'Easter' is 'Pâques'.

Total:

Quiz 2

Date: ...... / ...... / ......

1) What does 'au cours de Noël' mean in English?
2) True or false? 'Prier ensemble' means 'to pray alone'.
3) Give the French for 'Congratulations!'.
4) What does 'sous le sapin de Noël' mean in English?
5) How do you say 'fireworks' in French?
6) Give the name for two different places of worship in French.
7) Translate into French: 'Eid al-Fitr marks the end of the month of Ramadan.'
8) Translate into French: 'My friend told me a joke.'
9) What is 'une bûche de Noël' in English?
10) Give the French for 'the king' and 'the queen'.

Total:

Mixed Practice Quizzes

Quiz 3

Date: ...... / ...... / ......

1) How do you say 'atheist' in French?
2) What does this sentence mean in English?
   'Une brioche en forme de couronne s'appelle un 'gâteau des rois'.'
3) Translate into French: 'The fourteenth of July is very impressive.'
4) How do you say 'the extended family' in French?
5) Translate into French: 'People celebrate Hanukkah for eight days.'
6) In French, explain what people do with paper fish on 1st April in France.
7) Give the French for 'a procession'.
8) How do you say 'in a large part of France' in French?
9) Translate into English: 'Nous ouvrons les cadeaux le jour de Noël.'
10) What does 'de l'aube au coucher du soleil' mean in English?

Total:

Quiz 4

Date: ...... / ...... / ......

1) Translate into French: 'We eat turkey or goose for dinner.'
2) Give the French for 'bank holiday'.
3) Translate into English: 'J'ai trouvé la fève cachée dans la galette.'
4) What does 'prendre de bonnes résolutions' mean in English?
5) What does this sentence mean in English?
   'La fête nationale est un événement que beaucoup de gens célèbrent.'
6) What is 'New Year's Day' in French?
7) What does the verb 'se rendre compte' mean in English?
8) True or false? 'Valentine's Day' is 'la Saint-Sylvestre' in French.
9) What does 'échanger des cadeaux' mean in English?
10) Translate into French: 'People do traditional dances.'

Total:

Talking About Where You Live

First Go: ...../...../.....

En ville

	market	la boulangerie	
	supermarket		butcher's
la poste			library
	newsagent's	la gare ( )	(bus) station

J'habite dans une ville ....
I live .... in the countryside.

Je .... habiter dans ....
I prefer living in a city.

À l'avenir, je voudrais habiter soit au bord de la mer soit ....
........................., I'd like to live either .... or in the mountains.

Parle-moi de ta ville

Le système de transports en commun ... ...et aide à réduire et en ville.	The system works well... ...and the traffic and the noise in the town.
À cause des fréquents,... ...le centre-ville une zone piétonne.	Because of regular traffic jams,... ...the will become a .

Ma ville serait .... s'il y avait ....
My town .... almost perfect if there were a theatre.

Dans ma ville, il y a un .... et de nombreux magasins.
In my town, there's a big shopping centre and ....

Il n'y a pas .... dans ma ville. .... cinéma, par exemple.
There isn't a lot to do in my town. There's no cinema, for example.

Second Go:
..... / ..... / .....

Talking About Where You Live

En ville

	market		bakery
	supermarket		butcher's
	post office		library
	newsagent's		(bus) station

I live in a town in the countryside.

I prefer living in a city.

In the future, I'd like to live either by the sea or in the mountains.

Parle-moi de ta ville

	The public transport system works well... ...and helps to reduce the traffic and the noise in the town.
	Because of regular traffic jams,... ...the town centre will become a pedestrian zone.

My town would be almost perfect if there were a theatre.

In my town, there's a big shopping centre and numerous shops.

There isn't a lot to do in my town. There's no cinema, for example.

The Home

First Go: ..... /..... /.....

La maison

....	*furniture*	....	*bed*
....	*cupboard*	le bureau	....
l'armoire *(f)*	....	....	*oven*
....	*chair*	le lave-vaisselle	....

J'habite dans ....mais j' .... dans une ferme.	I live in a terraced house... ...but I used to live on ....
Dans ma maison individuelle, ...mais on n'a pas de	In my .... , there are six rooms... ...but we don't have a dining room.
Ma .... a une grande baie vitrée.	My bedroom has a large ....
J'habite dans un immeuble... ...qui se trouve	I live in a ....which is situated in the town centre.

C'est comment chez toi?

J'habite dans .... Je n'ai jamais déménagé.
I live in a council house. I've never ....

'HLM' = 'habitation à .... '

J'ai .... dans .... l'hiver dernier.
I moved into a flat ....

J'aime habiter dans une maison jumelée. C'est dans .... avec ....
I like living in a .... It's in a quiet area with a picturesque sea view.

La cuisine est au .... et il y a .... au premier étage.
The kitchen is on the ground floor and there's a bathroom ....

Nous avons un canapé confortable qui est dans ....
We have a .... which is in the living room.

Second Go: ...../...../.....

The Home

La maison

	furniture		bed
	cupboard		desk
	wardrobe		oven
	chair		dishwasher

	I live in a terraced house... ...but I used to live on a farm.
	In my detached house, there are six rooms... ...but we don't have a dining room.
	My bedroom has a large bay window.
	I live in a block of flats... ...which is situated in the town centre.

C'est comment chez toi?

'HLM' = '..'

I live in a council house. I've never moved house.

I moved into a flat last winter.

I like living in a semi-detached house. It's in a quiet area with a picturesque sea view.

The kitchen is on the ground floor and there's a bathroom on the first floor.

We have a comfortable sofa which is in the living room.

What You Do at Home

First Go: ..... /..... /.....

Une journée typique

______ pendant une journée typique?	What do you do during ______?
Je ______ à sept heures... ...et je quitte la maison ______ d'une heure.	I get up at seven o'clock... ...and I ______ the house in less than an hour.
Je fais le lit, puis je me lave et je ______.	I ______, then I ______ and I get dressed.
Je ______ après avoir pris le petit-déjeuner.	I brush my teeth after having eaten ______.
Je me douche avant de ______.	I ______ before going to bed.

Les tâches ménagères

______ *to cook*

nettoyer ______

mettre la table ______ *the table*

______ la voiture *to wash the car*

passer ______ *to vacuum*

faire du ______ *to do some gardening*

faire du bricolage *to do some* ______

______ les enfants *to look after children / to babysit*

Je fais ______ et je range la cuisine ______ par semaine.
I do the washing up and I ______ several times a week.

Parfois, j'aide ma mère à ______ le week-end.
Sometimes, ______ my mum bake at weekends.

Mes parents ______ et la lessive en rentrant du travail.
My parents do the shopping and the ______ once they get back from work.

Je dois faire certaines ______ pour gagner mon argent de poche.
I have to do certain chores ______.

Je n'achète rien avec l'argent car je veux ______.
I don't buy ______ with the money because I want to save it.

Second Go: ..... /..... /.....

What You Do at Home

Une journée typique

	What do you do during a typical day?
	I get up at seven o'clock... ...and I leave the house in less than an hour.
	I make the bed, then I wash and I get dressed.
	I brush my teeth after having eaten breakfast.
	I have a shower before going to bed.

Les tâches ménagères

	to cook		*to vacuum*
	to clean		*to do some gardening*
	to lay the table		*to do some DIY*
	to wash the car		*to look after children / to babysit*

I do the washing up and I tidy the kitchen several times a week.

Sometimes, I help my mum bake at weekends.

My parents do the shopping and the laundry once they get back from work.

I have to do certain chores to earn my pocket money.

I don't buy anything with the money because I want to save it.

 ✓  ✓  ✓

Mixed Practice Quizzes

I hope those pages weren't too much of a chore — here are a few quizzes on p.61-66 for you to try. Give yourself a mark out of ten to see how you've done.

Quiz 1

Date: ...... / ...... / ......

1) How do you say 'the ground floor' in French?
2) Give the French for 'newsagent's'.
3) Translate into English: 'Je me brosse les dents avant de m'habiller.'
4) What does this sentence mean in English?
   'Il y a beaucoup d'embouteillages et de bruit en ville.'
5) True or false? The verb 'emménager' means 'to move house'.
6) Translate into French: 'I make my bed after having eaten breakfast.'
7) What is 'un canapé' in English?
8) Translate into French: 'There's lots to do in my town.'
9) What is 'une zone piétonne' in English?
10) Give the French for two different chores.

Total:

Quiz 2

Date: ...... / ...... / ......

1) Translate into French: 'I want to save my pocket money.'
2) What is 'une baie vitrée' in English?
3) True or false? 'La boulangerie' means 'the butcher's'.
4) Give the French for 'to get back from work'.
5) Translate into French:
   'I would like to live either in the countryside or in the mountains.'
6) Name three different types of furniture in French.
7) Translate into English: 'Je fais du jardinage et du bricolage.'
8) Give the French for 'a council house'.
9) What is 'la circulation' in English?
10) Answer this question with two sentences in French:
    'Qu'est-ce que tu fais le matin?'

Total:

Mixed Practice Quizzes

Quiz 3

Date: ...... / ...... / ......

1) Translate into French: 'I used to live in a terraced house.'
2) What does this sentence mean in English?
   'Ma ville serait mieux s'il y avait un cinéma.'
3) True or false? 'Nettoyer la table' means 'to lay the table'.
4) Translate into English:
   'Les transports en commun dans ma ville marchent bien.'
5) Give two sentences in French to describe your home.
6) What does 'la lessive' mean in English?
7) Translate into English: 'Nous avons déménagé l'été dernier.'
8) Give the French for 'a bus station'.
9) Translate into French: 'My bedroom has a large wardrobe and a desk.'
10) What does the verb 'ranger' mean in English?

Total:

Quiz 4

Date: ...... / ...... / ......

1) How do you say 'I leave the house' in French?
2) Translate into French: 'There's a market and numerous shops.'
3) Give the English for 'au premier étage'.
4) What does this sentence mean in English?
   'Je fais certaines tâches ménagères pour gagner de l'argent.'
5) True or false? 'Il n'y a aucune bibliothèque' means
   'there is only one library'.
6) What does 'faire les courses' mean in English?
7) What does this sentence mean in English?
   'J'ai emménagé dans un quartier calme.'
8) Give the French for 'a city'.
9) Translate into English: 'J'aime habiter dans un appartement.'
10) What is the French infinitive of the verb 'to get up'?

Total:

Clothes Shopping

First Go: ..... /..... /.....

Faire les magasins

	clothes	l'imperméable *(m)*	
la marque		le pull	*hoodie*
la mode			*trousers*
	socks		*jeans*
les baskets *(f)*		les gants *(m)*	
	shirt		*the right size*
	T-shirt	le vendeur / la vendeuse	

Je ______ . *I'm browsing.* Ce sera tout? ______

Autre ______ ? *Anything else?* Ce sera tout. ______

J'aimerais bien des ______ .	I ______ some black shoes.
Je ______ un pyjama bleu.	I'm looking for ______ .
J'adore ______ en vitrine. Je peux ______ ?	I love the scarf ______ . Can I try it on?
Est-ce que vous avez cette ______ ?	______ this dress in red?
Et ______ en taille moyenne?	And do you have it in a ______ ?

À la caisse

.... est .... Elle coûte vingt euros, ce qui est bon marché.
The jacket is in the sale. It costs twenty euros, which is ....

Voulez-vous payer .... ou en espèces?
Do you want .... by bank card or .... ?

Ce manteau n'a aucune étiquette. .... ?
This .... doesn't have a .... How much is it?

Je voudrais échanger .... contre un chapeau. Voici ....
I would like to .... this jumper for .... Here is the receipt.

Cette jupe .... Je préférerais me faire rembourser.
This .... doesn't suit me. I would prefer ....

Second Go: ..... /..... /.....

Clothes Shopping

Faire les magasins

clothes	raincoat
brand	hoodie
fashion	trousers
socks	jeans
trainers	gloves
shirt	the right size
T-shirt	/ shop assistant
I'm browsing.	Is that everything?
Anything else?	That's all.

	I would like some black shoes.
	I'm looking for blue pyjamas.
	I love the scarf in the window. Can I try it on?
	Do you have this dress in red?
	And do you have it in a medium size?

À la caisse

The jacket is in the sale. It costs twenty euros, which is good value.

Do you want to pay by bank card or in cash?

This coat doesn't have a label. How much is it?

I would like to exchange this jumper for a hat. Here is the receipt.

This skirt doesn't suit me. I would prefer to get a refund.

More Shopping

First Go: ..... / ..... / .....

Au magasin

	shopping		a gram		a slice
la moitié		une boîte			sliced
	quarter		a packet		to weigh
	half a litre	un morceau			

Nous .... une petite portion de flan.
We would like ....

Most quantities are always followed by '.........' — 'encore' is an exception.

Voulez-vous .... ?
Would you like a litre of milk?

Je voudrais .... pain.
I would like more ....

Je pourrais avoir ...., s'il vous plaît?
.... *a kilogram of cheese, please?*

Faire des courses en ligne

C'est ______ de faire des courses en ligne,... ...mais j'aime pouvoir toucher et voir ______ .	It's convenient to ______ ,... ...but I like being able to touch and see what I'm buying.
Il est difficile pour ______ ______ de faire concurrence... ...aux ______ en ligne.	It's difficult for small shops ______ ... ...with big businesses ______ .
J' ______ des légumes en ligne... ...mais ils étaient abîmés.	I bought some vegetables ______ ... ...but they were ______ .
Je préfère acheter ______ en ligne... ...parce qu'ils sont ______ ... ...et ______ sont souvent réduits.	I prefer to buy clothes ______ ... ...because they're delivered quickly... ...and the prices are often ______ .

Second Go:
..... /..... /.....

More Shopping

Au magasin

shopping	a gram	a slice
half	a box	sliced
quarter	a packet	to weigh
half a litre	a piece	

Most .... are always followed by '............' — '..............................' is an exception.

We would like a small portion of flan.

Would you like a litre of milk?

I would like more bread.

Could I have a kilogram of cheese, please?

Faire des courses en ligne

	It's convenient to shop online,... ...but I like being able to touch and see what I'm buying.
	It's difficult for small shops to compete... ...with big businesses online.
	I bought some vegetables online... ...but they were damaged.
	I prefer to buy clothes online... ...because they're delivered quickly... ...and the prices are often reduced.

Giving and Asking for Directions

First Go: ..... / ..... / .....

Où est... ?

.... est juste ...., donc ce n'est pas loin d'ici.
The station is just over there, so it's not ....

La boulangerie est juste .... école et la banque .... de l'autre côté de la place.
The bakery is right next to the school and the bank is .... of the square.

Le village est .... de la ville. La ville est dans ....
The village is south-west of the town. The town is in the south of the country.

La poste est .... Elle se trouve .... l'église, ... l'hôpital et l'hôtel de ville.
The post office is nearby. .... *opposite the church, between the hospital and* ....

le nord	________
le sud	________
l'est *(m)*	________
l'ouest *(m)*	________

C'est loin d'ici?

________ au carrefour.	Turn left at the ________.
________ au rond-point... ...puis ________ la première rue à droite.	Go straight ahead at the ________... ...then take the first street ________.
________ le panneau 'toutes directions'... ...et allez ________ feux de signalisation.	Follow ________ for '________'... ...and go up to the ________.
Ne ________ pas le pont... ...parce que vous ________ payer un péage.	Don't cross ________... ...because you have to pay ________.
Faites attention car la rue n'a pas ________.	________ as the street doesn't have any pavements.

Second Go:
..... /..... /.....

Giving and Asking for Directions

Où est... ?

	north
	south
	east
	west

The station is just over there, so it's not far from here.

The bakery is right next to the school and the bank is on the opposite side of the square.

The village is south-west of the town. The town is in the south of the country.

The post office is nearby. It's situated opposite the church, between the hospital and town hall.

C'est loin d'ici?

	Turn left at the crossroads.
	Go straight ahead at the roundabout... ...then take the first street on the right.
	Follow the sign for 'all directions'... ...and go up to the traffic lights.
	Don't cross the bridge... ...because you have to pay a toll.
	Be careful as the street doesn't have any pavements.

Weather

First Go: ..... /..... /.....

Le temps

	It is...		*It is...*
du vent		chaud	
du	*sunny*		*cold*
du	*foggy*	beau	
			bad weather

	There is / are...		
des	*lightning*	en	*in winter*
du tonnerre		au	*in spring*
des	*storms*	en	*in summer*
des averses		en	*in autumn*
des	*bright spells*		

La météo

Hier, c'était .... et il a neigé.
Si on a de la chance, le temps .... plus tard.
Yesterday, it was cloudy and ....
.................................., the weather will be mild later.

Demain, ce sera ....
Tomorrow, it will be sunnier.

Il .... le matin, mais au cours de la journée
le temps deviendra ....
It will be cold in the morning, but ....
the weather will become stormier.

Ce matin, il y aura ....
et il gèlera. Il restera .... le soir.
This morning, there will be storms
and it .... It will
remain overcast in the evening.

Le climat ici est généralement
.................., mais aujourd'hui il pleut.
The .... here is usually
dry, but ....

Second Go:
...../...../.....

Weather

Le temps

It is...
windy
sunny
foggy

It is...
hot
cold
fine
bad weather

There is / are...
lightning
thunder
storms
showers
bright spells

in winter
in spring
in summer
in autumn

La météo

Yesterday, it was cloudy and it snowed. If we're lucky, the weather will be mild later.

Tomorrow, it will be sunnier.

It will be cold in the morning, but during the day the weather will become stormier.

This morning, there will be storms and it will freeze. It will remain overcast in the evening.

The climate here is usually dry, but today it's raining.

Mixed Practice Quizzes

There was a lot of info on those last few pages. These quizzes cover p.69-76 — give each of them a go to make sure that you're headed in the right direction.

Quiz 1

Date: ...... / ...... / ......

1) Translate into French: 'I'm browsing.'
2) What does 'la boulangerie est juste là-bas' mean in English?
3) Translate into French:
   'Small shops have to compete with big businesses online.'
4) How do you say 'the weather is stormy' in French?
5) True or false? The French for 'shoes' is 'les chaussures'.
6) Give the French for 'reduced'.
7) Translate into French: 'There is a toll to cross the bridge.'
8) How do you ask to try something on in French?
9) What does the verb 'peser' mean in English?
10) Translate into French: 'The climate here is quite mild.'

Total:

Quiz 2

Date: ...... / ...... / ......

1) Translate into French: 'Next week, it will be sunnier.'
2) Give the French for 'pavement'.
3) Translate into English:
   'Je peux payer en espèces ou par carte bancaire.'
4) What does 'abîmé' mean in English?
5) Give the four points of the compass in French.
6) What does this sentence mean in English?
   'Le temps deviendra plus nuageux au cours de la journée.'
7) True or false? 'Allez tout droit' means 'go straight ahead'.
8) How do you say 'they're delivered quickly' in French?
9) What does 'en solde' mean in English?
10) Translate into French: 'It's not far from here.'

Total:

Mixed Practice Quizzes

Quiz 3

Date: ...... / ...... / ......

1) What does this sentence mean in English? 'Ça ne me va pas.'
2) Give the names of all four seasons in French.
3) What does this sentence mean in English?
'La banque est située entre l'église et l'école.'
4) Translate into French: 'It was overcast yesterday.'
5) How do you say 'half a litre of milk' in French?
6) Translate into French: 'Do you have it in a medium size?'
7) True or false? 'Il y aura des éclairs' means
'there will be bright spells'.
8) Translate into French: 'Take the first street on the right.'
9) What is 'un ticket de caisse' in English?
10) Translate into English: 'L'hôtel de ville se trouve en face de l'hôpital.'

Total:

Quiz 4

Date: ...... / ...... / ......

1) Give the French for four different types of clothing.
2) What does this sentence mean in English?
'Faites attention — il n'y a pas de feux de signalisation.'
3) Translate into English: 'Si on de la chance, il fera beau plus tard.'
4) What does this mean in English?
'Je cherche un imperméable jaune.'
5) True or false? The French for 'half' is 'la moitié'.
6) What does 'tournez à gauche' mean in English?
7) Translate into English: 'Hier, il y avait du brouillard.'
8) What does this sentence mean in English?
'Je pourrais avoir une boîte de chocolats, s'il vous plaît?'
9) Give the French for 'a label'.
10) Translate into English: 'J'aime pouvoir toucher et voir ce que j'achète.'

Total:

Healthy Living

First Go: ..... / ..... / .....

Manger sainement

Je garde la forme en mangeant... by eating...	... .balanced meals.
	...peu de gras. ... .
	...peu de sucre. ... .

J'ai ...... à manger au moins cinq fruits et ...... par jour ce mois-ci.
I've succeeded in eating ...... five fruits and vegetables ....

J'essaie de cultiver les bonnes habitudes en mangeant la nourriture bio et ....
I try to cultivate ...... by eating ...... and drinking plenty of water.

Mon père a fait un régime pour perdre du poids.
My father .... to ....

Pour rester en bonne santé

...... pour rester en bonne santé?
What do you do to ......?

Je ...... au lieu de l'ascenseur pour faire plus d'exercice.
I take the stairs rather than ...... to do ....

Parfois, je vais au collège ...... ou ....

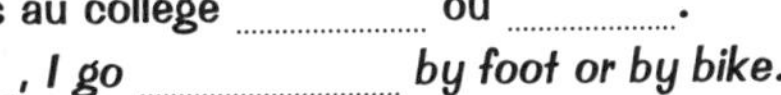

......, I go ...... by foot or by bike.

...... pour te détendre?
What do you do to ......?

Je ...... en sortant avec mes amis ....
I relax by ...... with my friends in the evenings.

Second Go: ..... /..... /.....

Healthy Living

Manger sainement

I stay in shape by eating...	...balanced meals.
	...little fat.
	...little sugar.

I've succeeded in eating at least five fruits and vegetables a day this month.

I try to cultivate good habits by eating organic food and drinking plenty of water.

My father went on a diet to lose weight.

Pour rester en bonne santé

What do you do to stay healthy?

I take the stairs rather than the lift to do more exercise.

Sometimes, I go to school by foot or by bike.

What do you do to relax?

I relax by going out with my friends in the evenings.

Unhealthy Living

First Go: ..... /..... /.....

Le tabagisme

Beaucoup de gens .... arrêter de fumer .... du mal à respirer.
Many people want .... smoking because they have .....

Le tabagisme cause des .... comme le cancer du poumon et ....
.. causes serious illnesses like .... and heart attacks.

.... peuvent aider les gens à cesser de fumer.
E-cigarettes .... people ....

Les drogues

Il faut aider ceux .... accros aux drogues.
We must .... who are ....

On devrait .... le public aux dangers des substances qui créent une dépendance.
We should increase awareness amongst the public of .....

On doit avertir ceux qui .... parce que c'est .... pour la santé.
We ought .... those who take drugs because it is bad for ....

Est-ce que les jeunes boivent trop?

Ils .... le week-end.	They only drink at the weekend.
Beaucoup de jeunes boivent pour s'amuser... ...donc ils s'enivrent quand ils sortent en boîte.	Many .... drink ....so they .... when they ....
.... qu'ils ont besoin .... pour se détendre.	Some people say they need to be drunk ....
Je trouve ....car l'alcool a	I find alcoholism frightening... ...because alcohol has harmful effects.

Second Go:
...../...../.....

Unhealthy Living

Le tabagisme

Many people want to stop smoking because they have trouble breathing.

Smoking addiction causes serious illnesses like lung cancer and heart attacks.

E-cigarettes can help people give up smoking.

Les drogues

We must help those who are addicted to drugs.

We should increase awareness amongst the public of the dangers of addictive substances.

We ought to warn those who take drugs because it is bad for your health.

Est-ce que les jeunes boivent trop?

	They only drink at the weekend.
	Many young people drink to have fun... ...so they get drunk when they go clubbing.
	Some people say they need to be drunk to relax.
	I find alcoholism frightening... ...because alcohol has harmful effects.

Illnesses

First Go: ..... /..... /.....

Les maladies

tomber malade	
	to cure
	to vomit
la grippe	
l'obésité (f)	
	medicine
le comprimé	
/	doctor

Use plus a body part to say something hurts:

J' doigt.
My finger hurts.

J' gorge.
I have a sore throat.

J' pieds.
My feet hurt.

J' souvent ,... ...je tousse et j'ai le nez qui coule.	I often catch colds,... ...I and I get a .
Quand je ,... ... m'a donné .	When I was feeling unwell,... ...the doctor a prescription.
De temps en temps, je des choses et je .	, I worry about things and I feel depressed.

Des problèmes de santé

Le sida .... dans les pays en développement.
.... *remains a big problem in* ....

...., les jeunes s'inquiètent souvent de leurs poids et de ....
Because of the media, young people .... *about* .... *and their appearance.*

Il y a toujours de la pression pour .... et se conformer aux stéréotypes.
There's always .... *to be very thin and to* ....

Second Go: ..... /..... /.....

Illnesses

Les maladies

	to fall ill
	to cure
	to vomit
	flu
	obesity
	medicine
	tablet
/	doctor

Use plus a to say something hurts:

My finger hurts.

I have a sore throat.

My feet hurt.

	I often catch colds,... ...I cough and I get a runny nose.
	When I was feeling unwell,... ...the doctor gave me a prescription.
	From time to time, I worry about things and I feel depressed.

Des problèmes de santé

AIDS remains a big problem in developing countries.

Because of the media, young people often worry about their weight and their appearance.

There's always pressure to be very thin and to conform to stereotypes.

Mixed Practice Quizzes

Time for the next batch of quizzes — these ones test the content on p.79-84. Give them your best shot, then mark your answers to see how you've done.

Quiz 1

Date: ...... / ...... / ......

1) Give the French for: 'My arm hurts.'
2) Translate into English: 'La dépendance à l'alcool est une maladie.'
3) True or false? The French for 'a prescription' is 'un comprimé'.
4) In French, give one reason why smoking is bad for your health.
5) What is the French infinitive of the verb 'to vomit'?
6) Give one answer to this question in French: 'Qu'est-ce que tu fais pour rester en bonne santé?'
7) What does the phrase 'trop de gras' mean in English?
8) Translate into English: 'Les cigarettes électroniques peuvent aider ceux qui fument à arrêter.'
9) How do you say 'vegetables' in French?
10) What is 'un régime' in English?

Total:

Quiz 2

Date: ...... / ...... / ......

1) How do you say 'I stay in shape' in French?
2) Translate into English: 'Elle est tombée malade dimanche soir.'
3) Answer this question with a sentence in French: 'Qu'est-ce que tu fais pour te détendre?'
4) What does the verb 'cesser' mean in English?
5) Give two ways of saying 'doctor' in French.
6) What does this sentence mean in English? 'Il a du mal à respirer.'
7) What is 'le sida' in English?
8) Translate into French: 'We should help those who are addicted to alcohol.'
9) What does 'à cause des médias' mean in English?
10) Give the French for 'a serious illness'.

Total:

Mixed Practice Quizzes

Quiz 3

Date: ...... / ...... / ......

1) Translate into French: 'Smoking addiction has harmful effects.'
2) What does 'perdre du poids' mean in English?
3) How do you say 'organic food' in French?
4) True or false? 'Il prend l'ascenseur au lieu des escaliers' means 'he takes the stairs instead of the lift'.
5) How do you say 'les substances qui créent une dépendance' in English?
6) What does 'être ivre' mean in English?
7) Translate into English: 'Je m'inquiète de mon apparence et mon poids.'
8) What is 'le cancer du poumon' in English?
9) Translate into French: 'It is important to eat balanced meals.'
10) What does this sentence mean in English? 'Il faut sensibiliser les jeunes aux dangers d'alcool.'

Total:

Quiz 4

Date: ...... / ...... / ......

1) Give the French for 'heart attack'.
2) Translate into French: 'We must drink lots of water.'
3) What is the French infinitive of the verb 'to warn'?
4) What are 'un rhume' and 'la grippe' in English?
5) Translate into French: 'He gets drunk at the weekend.'
6) What does the verb 'se droguer' mean in English?
7) Translate into English: 'L'obésité reste un grand problème.'
8) How do you say 'good habits' in French?
9) Translate into English: 'Parfois, elle se sent déprimée.'
10) True or false? The French infinitive 'guérir' means 'to cure'.

Total:

Environmental Problems

First Go: ..... /..... /.....

Ce n'est pas écologique

______ est un gaspillage... ...des ressources naturelles de la Terre. ...des ______ .	Packaging is ______ ... ...of the Earth's ______ . ...of raw materials.
______ peut ______ à se décomposer.	A plastic bag can take years to ______ .
______ peuvent ______ les rivières avec des produits chimiques nocifs.	Factories can pollute ______ with ______ .
______ peut provoquer des ______ .	Air pollution ______ health problems.
______ contribue à l'effet de serre... ...et mène ______ des écosystèmes.	Deforestation ______ to the ______ ... ...and leads to the loss of ecosystems.
Le gaz d'échappement cause ______ de la Terre.	______ cause global warming.
On détruit ______ .	We're ______ the ozone layer.

Protéger la planète

Il faut réduire la production de .... et augmenter ....
We must .... the production of carbon dioxide and .... the number of trees.

Il faut .... les espèces qui sont ....
We need to protect .... that are threatened by extinction.

On doit remplacer le charbon et .... avec ....
We must replace .... and oil with renewable energy.

Nous .... de l'eau dans .... Il est important de l'économiser car seulement .... de l'eau sur la planète est potable.
We waste water in everyday life. It's important to .... because only one percent of water .... is ....

Second Go:
..... /..... /.....

Environmental Problems

Ce n'est pas écologique

	Packaging is a waste... ...of the Earth's natural resources. ...of raw materials.
	A plastic bag can take years to decompose.
	Factories can pollute rivers with harmful chemicals.
	Air pollution can cause health problems.
	Deforestation contributes to the greenhouse effect... ...and leads to the loss of ecosystems.
	Exhaust fumes cause global warming.
	We're destroying the ozone layer.

Protéger la planète

We must reduce the production of carbon dioxide and increase the number of trees.

We need to protect species that are threatened by extinction.

We must replace coal and oil with renewable energy.

We waste water in everyday life. It's important to save it because only one percent of water on the planet is drinkable.

Problems in Society

First Go: ..... /..... /.....

La violence chez les jeunes

________ à la maison... ...j'ai ________. ...quelqu'un ________ et volé mon portable. ...j'ai ________ par un voyou.	On the way home... ...I was attacked. ...someone threatened me and ________ my ________. ...I was hit by ________.
J'ai peur des ________ dans mon quartier.	________ of the gangs in my ________.
On ________ et on se moque de moi au collège.	People harass me and ________ ________ at school.

L'inégalité sociale

.... entre .... et .... peut provoquer des émeutes violentes.
Social inequality between the rich and the poor can provoke ....

La pauvreté est ....
Poverty is a serious global problem.

Il faut aider ....
We must .... vulnerable people.

.... doivent donner la priorité à la question de ....
Politicians .... the issue of social equality.

Les sans-abri

'le SDF' = 'sans .... fixe' (homeless people)

.... sont souvent ....
Homeless people are often socially excluded.

Si on est au chômage, on n'a pas .... de ....
Cependant, il n'est pas possible de .... sans .... fixe.
If people are ...., they can't afford to pay for accommodation.
However, it is not possible to find a job without a permanent address.

Second Go: ..... /..... /.....

Problems in Society

La violence chez les jeunes

	On the way home... ...I was attacked. ...someone threatened me and stole my phone. ...I was hit by a hooligan.
	I'm scared of the gangs in my neighbourhood.
	People harass me and make fun of me at school.

L'inégalité sociale

Social inequality between the rich and the poor can provoke violent riots.

Poverty is a serious global problem.

We must help vulnerable people.

Politicians must prioritise the issue of social equality.

Les sans-abri

Homeless people are often socially excluded.

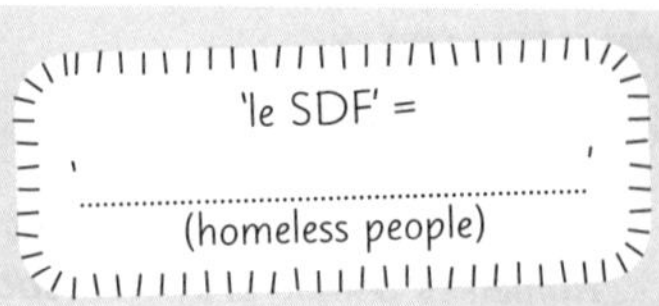

If people are unemployed, they can't afford to pay for accommodation. However, it is not possible to find a job without a permanent address.

Problems in Society

First Go: ..... /..... /.....

Les effets de la guerre

______ de gens ont été ______ ou grièvement blessés pendant la guerre.	Hundreds of people were killed or ______ during ______.
Les guerres ______ ... ...à ______. ...au ______. ...à beaucoup ______.	______ have led... ...to destruction. ...to the displacement of refugees. ...to many deaths.
Les gens ont fréquemment ______ ... ...leurs ______. ...tous leurs biens.	People have often lost... ...their homes. ...all their ______.
Il y a eu ______ et ______ a été harcelée.	There have been attacks and the civilians have been ______.

Les catastrophes naturelles

Le gouvernement .... pour aider .... du tremblement de terre.
The .... is taking measures to help the victims of the ....

Des milliers de personnes ont dû .... après .... l'année dernière qui ont causé de gros dégâts.
.... of people had to leave their homes after the floods last year that caused ....

.... a ravagé le village et c'était une expérience ....
A fire .... the village and it was a frightening experience.

Il est important que .... soient protégés contre ....
It is important that inhabitants .... natural disasters.

Second Go:
...... /...... /......

Problems in Society

Les effets de la guerre

	Hundreds of people were killed or seriously injured during the war.
	Wars have led... ...to destruction. ...to the displacement of refugees. ...to many deaths.
	People have often lost... ...their homes. ...all their possessions.
	There have been attacks and the civilians have been harassed.

Les catastrophes naturelles

The government is taking measures to help the victims of the earthquake.

Thousands of people had to leave their homes after the floods last year that caused serious damage.

A fire devastated the village and it was a frightening experience.

It is important that inhabitants are protected from natural disasters.

Contributing to Society

First Go: ..... /..... /.....

Être écologique

Les gens .... des choses recyclables comme le papier et le verre dans ....
People throw .... like .... and .... in the bin.

J'essaie .... en achetant les produits bio.
I try to be green by buying ....

Je .... toujours de trier mes .... quand je fais du recyclage.
I always remember .... my rubbish when I ....

Pour ...., il faut .... quand on quitte la maison.
To save energy, you must switch off the lights when you ....

Si chacun prenait une ou deux mesures pour .... le gaspillage des ressources, nous pourrions ....
If .... does one or two things to combat ...., we could save the planet.

Aider les autres

Tu aimes aider .... ?	Do you like helping others?
Dans mon ....je fais du travail bénévole... ...pour	In my free time... ...I do ....for a charity.
Je vais ....pour aider	I am going to lead a campaign... ...to help refugees.
En travaillant ensemble... ...nous pouvons .... la vie des gens défavorisés.	By ....we can improve the lives of ....
C'est un grand défi... ...mais	It's a ....but it's worthwhile.

Second Go: ..... /..... /.....

Contributing to Society

Être écologique

People throw recyclable things like paper and glass in the bin.

I try to be green by buying green products.

I always remember to sort my rubbish when I recycle.

To save energy, you must switch off the lights when you leave the house.

If each person does one or two things to combat the waste of resources, we could save the planet.

Aider les autres

	Do you like helping others?
	In my free time... ...I do voluntary work... ...for a charity.
	I am going to lead a campaign... ...to help refugees.
	By working together... ...we can improve the lives of disadvantaged people.
	It's a big challenge... ...but it's worthwhile.

Mixed Practice Quizzes

Give these quizzes a go to check you've got the hang of these weighty subjects. The quizzes cover the stuff on p.87-94 — mark each one to see how you've done.

Quiz 1

Date: ...... / ...... / ......

1) How do you say 'I do voluntary work' in French?
2) Translate into English: 'La population civile a dû quitter le village.'
3) What does 'ça vaut la peine' mean in English?
4) True or false? The French verb 'se moquer' means 'to make fun'.
5) How do you say 'hundreds of people' in French?
6) What does this sentence mean in English? 'Les usines font des produits chimiques nocifs.'
7) Give two ways of saying 'the homeless' in French.
8) What does the phrase 'trier les déchets' mean in English?
9) Give the French for 'natural disasters'.
10) Translate into French: 'Packaging is a waste of raw materials.'

Total:

Quiz 2

Date: ...... / ...... / ......

1) What does 'menacé d'extinction' mean in English?
2) Translate into English: 'J'ai été agressé en sortant du collège.'
3) What does this sentence mean in English? 'Il est impossible de trouver un emploi sans domicile fixe.'
4) True or false? The French for 'drinkable' is 'potable'.
5) How do you say 'exhaust fumes' in French?
6) Translate into English: 'L'inégalité sociale est un grave problème mondial.'
7) Give the French for 'a charity'.
8) What does the French verb 'provoquer' mean in English?
9) Give the French for 'refugees'.
10) Translate into French: 'A lot of people have lost their homes.'

Total:

Mixed Practice Quizzes

Quiz 3

Date: ...... / ...... / ......

1) Translate into French: 'A gang threatened me.'
2) How do you say 'the greenhouse effect' in French?
3) What does 'les émeutes violentes' mean in English?
4) Translate into English: 'Une inondation a détruit le village — c'était une expérience effrayante.'
5) What does 'les produits bio' mean in English?
6) Translate into French: 'Deforestation contributes to global warming.'
7) In French, give one thing you can do to protect the environment.
8) Translate into French: 'We must help homeless people.'
9) True or false? The French for 'possessions' is 'les biens'.
10) What does this sentence mean in English? 'Les incendies l'année dernière avait causé de gros dégâts.'

Total:

Quiz 4

Date: ...... / ...... / ......

1) What does 'donner la priorité à la question' mean in English?
2) Translate into French: 'I always remember to switch off the lights when I leave the house.'
3) Give the French for 'earthquake'.
4) What does this sentence mean in English? 'Nous pouvons améliorer la vie des réfugiés.'
5) Translate into French: 'We must combat the waste of resources.'
6) What does 'le gaz carbonique' mean in English?
7) In French, give one example of how war can affect people.
8) Translate into English: 'La pollution de l'eau peut mener à la perte des écosystèmes.'
9) How do you say 'the government is taking measures' in French?
10) What does 'un voyou' mean in English?

Total:

Where to Go

First Go: ..... /..... /.....

Les pays du monde

____	England
____	Great Britain
____	United States
l'Allemagne *(f)*	____
le Brésil	____
____	China
l'Espagne *(f)*	____
____	Russia
la Belgique	____
la Suisse	Switzerland
____	India

l'Afrique *(f)*	____
l'Amérique *(f)*	____
____	Asia
____	Europe
à l'étranger	____
____	sea
____	beach
____	the Mediterranean

Je vais .... Canada.
I'm going to Canada.

Je vais .... Pays-Bas.
I'm going to the Netherlands.

Je vais .... Algérie.
I'm going to Algeria.

____ for masc. sing. countries

____ for plural countries

____ for fem. sing. countries and masc. sing. countries that begin with a vowel.

Les vacances

L'année dernière, je ____ au Japon.	Last year, I went to ____.
____, je vais aller ____ ____ avec ma famille.	This summer, I'm ____ to Northern Ireland with my family.
Nous visiterons des ____ à Paris... ...car ma mère ____ beaucoup à l'histoire.	____ historic sites in Paris... ...because my mum is really interested in ____.
Après ça, j' ____ au Pays de Galles pour trois jours.	After that, I'll go to ____ for three days.
Je voudrais aussi aller ____.	I would also like to go to Scotland.

Second Go: ..... /..... /.....

Where to Go

Les pays du monde

	England
	Great Britain
	United States
	Germany
	Brazil
	China
	Spain
	Russia
	Belgium
	Switzerland
	India

	Africa
	America
	Asia
	Europe
	abroad
	sea
	beach
	the Mediterranean

I'm going to Canada. ← ______ for ______ countries

I'm going to the Netherlands. ← ______ for ______ countries

I'm going to Algeria. ← ______ for ______ countries and ______ countries that ______

Les vacances

	Last year, I went to Japan.
	This summer, I'm going to go to Northern Ireland with my family.
	We'll visit historic sites in Paris... ...because my mum is really interested in history.
	After that, I'll go to Wales for three days.
	I would also like to go to Scotland.

Accommodation

First Go: ..... /..... /.....

Le logement

Est-ce qu'il y a .... au centre-ville?
Is there a luxury hotel in the ....?

Je .... une chambre d'hôte à Lyon qui ....
I'm looking for a .... in Lyon that isn't expensive.

Il cherche .... au bord de la mer.
He's looking for a campsite at the ....

Je préférerais .... dans ....
I would prefer to stay in a tent.

Où aimez-vous loger?

Quel est votre type de ________ préféré?	What is your favourite type of accommodation?
Je préfère ________ dans une auberge de jeunesse parce que... ...c'est ________ qu'un hôtel. ...j'aime ________ de nouvelles personnes.	I prefer staying in a ________ ________ because... ...it's less expensive than ________. ...I like getting to know ________.
J'aime ________ camping parce que... ... ________ me plaît. ...j'adore ________ la campagne. ...j' ________ la nature.	I like camping because... ...life in the open air ________. ...I love exploring the ________. ...I really like ________.
Je n'aime pas ________.	I don't like holiday camps.
On peut ________ plus ________ ________ dans un hôtel car... ...on ne doit pas ________. ...les chambres sont déjà préparées.	You can relax more if you stay in ________ because... ...you don't have to cook. ...the rooms are ________.

Second Go: ...../...../.....	# Accommodation

Le logement

Is there a luxury hotel in the town centre?

I'm looking for a bed and breakfast in Lyon that isn't expensive.

He's looking for a campsite at the seaside.

I would prefer to stay in a tent.

Où aimez-vous loger?

	What is your favourite type of accommodation?
	I prefer staying in a youth hostel because... ...it's less expensive than a hotel. ...I like getting to know new people.
	I like camping because... ...life in the open air pleases me. ...I love exploring the countryside. ...I really like nature.
	I don't like holiday camps.
	You can relax more if you stay in a hotel because... ...you don't have to cook. ...the rooms are already prepared.

Getting Ready to Go

First Go: ..... /..... /.....

Les préparatifs

J' ________ une chambre du 5 mai au 12 mai.	I booked ________ from 5th May to 12th May.
Nous ________ un camping-car pour deux semaines.	We're going to rent a ________ for two weeks.
Avez-vous ________ ?	Do you have ID?
J'ai mis mon passeport et mes ________ dans ma valise.	I put my ________ and my sunglasses in my ________ .
________ et les sacs de couchage sont dans ________ de la voiture.	The luggage and the ________ are in the boot of the car.

Faire une réservation

J'utiliserai .... pour faire une réservation.
I .... the travel agency ....

Je préférerais .... avec une piscine.
I would prefer a hotel in the mountains ....

Je voudrais réserver une chambre avec .... et une chambre à lits jumeaux.
I would like .... one room with a double bed and ....

Il veut rester dans une caravane avec des ....
He wants .... in .... with bunk beds.

Nous voudrions réserver .... pour .... du 13 juillet au 17 juillet. Nous sommes .... et un enfant.
We would like .... a pitch for one tent from 13th July to 17th July. We are two adults and ....

Je préfère une chambre simple avec .... qui donne sur la mer.
I prefer a .... with air conditioning which ....

Second Go:
..... /..... /.....

Getting Ready to Go

Les préparatifs

	I booked a room from 5th May to 12th May.
	We're going to rent a campervan for two weeks.
	Do you have ID?
	I put my passport and my sunglasses in my suitcase.
	The luggage and the sleeping bags are in the boot of the car.

Faire une réservation

I will use the travel agency to make a reservation.

I would prefer a hotel in the mountains with a pool.

I would like to book one room with a double bed and one room with twin beds.

He wants to stay in a caravan with bunk beds.

We would like to reserve a pitch for one tent from 13th July to 17th July. We are two adults and one child.

I prefer a single room with air conditioning which overlooks the sea.

How to Get There

First Go: ..... /..... /.....

Voyager

Use 'monter dans' to say '..............................' and 'descendre de' to say '..............................'.

Je suis monté dans .... à Bordeaux.
I .... the train in Bordeaux.

Je ...., mais je ne connais pas ....
I would drive, but I .... the way.

Je préfère les voitures .... car .... sont ....
I .... to buses because buses are not very reliable.

J'attends .... du TGV. J'ai regardé .... et il devrait arriver à six heures.
I'm waiting for the TGV to arrive. I looked at the timetable and it .... at six o'clock.

'TGV' = 'train à ....' (high-speed train)

Nous allons .... Selon ...., nous devons prendre l'autoroute.
We're going to hire a car. According to the map, we need to take ....

Nous .... le bateau.
We missed ....

En avion

Je suis arrivé ____ deux heures avant l'heure du départ.	I arrived at the airport two hours before the ____.
Cependant, ____ à cause d'un problème technique.	However, the flight was delayed due to ____.
J'ai enregistré ____.	I ____ my suitcase.
J'ai peur de voler parce que... ...mon imagination ____ ____ le pire.	I'm ____ because... ...I always imagine the worst.
____ sont si pratiques et ____.	Planes are so ____ and fast.

Second Go:
...... /...... /......

How to Get There

Voyager

I got on the train in Bordeaux.

Use '..............................' to say 'to get on' and '..............................' to say 'to get off'.

I would drive, but I don't know the way.

I prefer cars to buses because buses are not very reliable.

I'm waiting for the TGV to arrive. I looked at the timetable and it should arrive at six o'clock.

'TGV' = '.............................. ....' (high-speed train)

We're going to hire a car. According to the map, we need to take the motorway.

We missed the boat.

En avion

	I arrived at the airport two hours before the departure time.
	However, the flight was delayed due to a technical problem.
	I checked in my suitcase.
	I'm scared of flying because... ...I always imagine the worst.
	Planes are so convenient and fast.

What to Do

First Go: ..... /..... /.....

Le tourisme

l'office (*m*) de ______ — *tourist office*

les renseignements (*m*) — ______

______ — *tourist attraction*

le parc d'attractions — ______

______ — *castle*

la visite guidée — ______

______ — *town plan*

______ — *postcard*

En vacances...

J'ai visité .... et je suis allé à la plage.
I visited a cathedral and I went ....

J'ai décidé d'aller .... pour apprendre autant que possible .... C'était vraiment intéressant.
I decided to go to the museum .... as much as possible about the region. It was ....

L'un de mes plus grands plaisirs, c'est faire ....
One of .... is going on a boat tour.

Le zoo ....
C'était vraiment divertissant.
I liked .... a lot.
It was ....

J'aime aller .... avec ma famille après le dîner.
I like going to the fair with my family ....

J'achète toujours .... quand je vais en vacances.
I always buy a new swimming costume when ....

J'adore .... à la plage, donc je n'oublie jamais ....
I love sunbathing ...., so I never .... my suncream.

Second Go: ...../...../.....

What to Do

Le tourisme

tourist office
information
tourist attraction
theme park
castle
guided tour
town plan
postcard

En vacances...

I visited a cathedral and I went to the beach.

I decided to go to the museum to learn as much as possible about the region. It was really interesting.

One of my greatest pleasures is going on a boat tour.

I liked the zoo a lot.
It was really entertaining.

I like going to the fair with my family after dinner.

I always buy a new swimming costume when I go on holiday.

I love sunbathing at the beach, so I never forget my suncream.

Mixed Practice Quizzes

Before you start planning your dream holiday, have a go at these mixed quizzes. The tests cover the content on p.97-106 — look through the section to mark them.

Quiz 1

Date: ...... / ...... / ......

1) Translate into French: 'I bought a new swimming costume.'
2) Give two French verbs that mean 'to stay'.
3) How do you say 'a room with twin beds' in French?
4) Translate into French:
   'I arrived at the airport and checked in my suitcase.'
5) What does 'aller à l'étranger' mean in English?
6) True or false? 'Un hôtel de jeunesse' means 'a youth hostel'.
7) What does this sentence mean in English?
   'J'ai décidé d'aller à l'office de tourisme pour trouver des renseignements.'
8) What does the French verb 'louer' mean in English?
9) How do you say 'I went to Brazil' in French?
10) Translate into French: 'I got off the plane.'

Total:

Quiz 2

Date: ...... / ...... / ......

1) How do you say 'according to the timetable' in French?
2) Translate into French: 'Next year, I am going to the United States.'
3) How do you say 'a campsite' in French?
4) Translate into French: 'I forgot my suncream.'
5) True or false? 'Les trains son peu fiables' means
   'the trains aren't very reliable'.
6) Give the French for 'a guided tour'.
7) Translate into French: 'I have put the luggage in the boot of the car.'
8) Give the French for 'a holiday camp'.
9) What does the verb 'se détendre' mean in English?
10) Translate into French: 'The flight was delayed.'

Total:

Mixed Practice Quizzes

Quiz 3

Date: ...... / ...... / ......

1) What is the French infinitive of the verb 'to fly'?
2) Translate into English: 'Nous irons à la plage tous les jours.'
3) Answer this question with a sentence in French: 'Quel est votre type de logement préféré?'
4) Translate into French: 'It's less expensive than a hotel.'
5) What does this sentence mean in English? 'Nous avons réservé une chambre avec des lits superposés.'
6) Translate into French: 'I like to visit a cathedral when I go on holiday.'
7) What does the phrase 'en plein air' mean in English?
8) How do you say 'sleeping bags' in French?
9) Translate into English: 'Selon la carte, nous devons prendre l'autoroute.'
10) What is the French infinitive of the verb 'to sunbathe'?

Total:

Quiz 4

Date: ...... / ...... / ......

1) Give the English for 'un emplacement'.
2) Translate into English: 'Je préférerais rester dans un hôtel de luxe.'
3) What does this sentence mean in English? 'Je suis monté dans l'autobus pour visiter le château.'
4) Give the name of four continents in French.
5) What does this sentence mean in English? 'L'un de mes plus grands plaisirs, c'est aller à un parc d'attractions.'
6) Translate into French: 'I'm looking for a bed and breakfast in the town centre.'
7) How do you ask to reserve a single room with air conditioning in French?
8) Translate into French: 'Do you have ID?'
9) What does 'le musée m'a beaucoup plu' mean in English?
10) Translate into French: 'I will go to Germany for one week.'

Total:

School Subjects

First Go: ..... /..... /.....

J'aime...

'l'EPS' = 'l'éducation ...., et ....'

J'adore l'EPS! C'est chouette parce que je ne dois pas .... et j'aime bien faire de l'exercice.
I love ....! It's .... because I don't have to concentrate and I really like ....

J'aime assez les maths car c'est .... Cependant, je préfère la ....
I quite like .... because it's logical. However, I prefer English literature.

Je préfère .... d'instruction civique parce que .... est amusant.
I prefer .... lessons because the teacher is ....

J'ai un côté artistique, donc ma .... est .... En plus, ... sont toujours détendus.
I have an ...., so my favourite subject is art. In addition, the lessons are always ....

Je .... à la religion. Malheureusement, j'ai dû la .... pour étudier le français.
I was interested in .... *..............................,*
I had to drop it .... French.

Je n'aime pas...

À mon avis, ______ est horrible... ...car elle est trop ______ . ...parce que je n'aime pas faire les expériences.	In my opinion, physics is horrible... ...because it's too complicated. ...because I don't like ______ .
Je pense que ______ est ______ et ne sert à rien.	I think IT is boring and ______ .
Je trouve ______ plus difficile que la chimie.	I find modern languages harder than ______ .
Je n'aime pas ______ l'espagnol.	I don't like learning ______ .

Second Go:
..... /..... /.....

School Subjects

J'aime...

I love PE! It's great because I don't have to concentrate and I really like doing exercise.

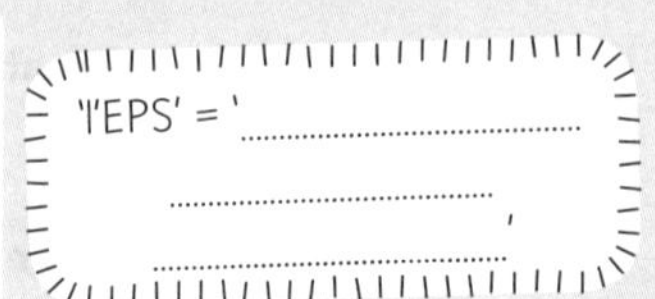

I quite like maths because it's logical. However, I prefer English literature.

I prefer citizenship lessons because the teacher is funny.

I have an artistic side, so my favourite subject is art. In addition, the lessons are always relaxed.

I was interested in religious studies. Unfortunately, I had to drop it to study French.

Je n'aime pas...

	In my opinion, physics is horrible... ...because it's too complicated. ...because I don't like doing the experiments.
	I think IT is boring and useless.
	I find modern languages harder than chemistry.
	I don't like learning Spanish.

School Routine

First Go: ..... /..... /.....

Aller à l'école

Comment vas-tu ______ ?	How do you get to school?
______ parce que j'habite près de l'école.	I walk there because I live ______ school.
Quand il pleut, ma mère ______ en voiture.	When ______, my mum takes me ______.

Une journée typique

______	*classroom*	le trimestre	______
l'emploi *(m)* du temps	______	______	*late*
______	*holidays*	de bonne heure	______
______	*return to school (after the summer)*	______	*every day*

.... commence à neuf heures, et elle finit à quinze heures.
The school day .... nine o'clock, and it .... at three pm.

Il y a deux .... et on prend le déjeuner à midi.
There are two twenty-minute breaks and we .... at midday.

J'ai .... chaque jour. Par contre, je ne fais qu'une heure .... par semaine.
I have a maths lesson .... On the other hand, I only do one hour of German a week.

C'est .... Si j'avais ...., je commencerais les cours plus tard.
It's a tiring day. If I had the choice, I .... lessons ....

Pendant la récré

D'habitude, je discute .... et nous mangeons le déjeuner.
...................., I talk with my friends and we ....

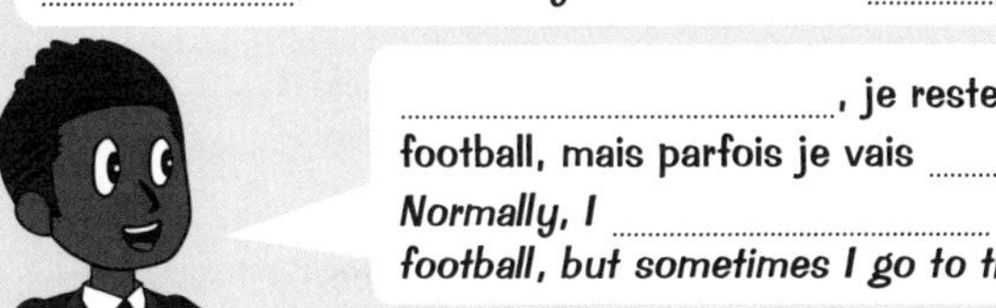

...................., je reste dehors et je joue au football, mais parfois je vais ....
Normally, I .... and I play football, but sometimes I go to the canteen.

Second Go: ..... /..... /.....

School Routine

Aller à l'école

	How do you get to school?
	I walk there because I live close to school.
	When it's raining, my mum takes me in the car.

Une journée typique

	classroom		*term*
	timetable		*late*
	holidays		*early*
	return to school (after the summer)		*every day*

The school day starts at nine o'clock, and it finishes at three pm.

There are two twenty-minute breaks and we have lunch at midday.

I have a maths lesson every day. On the other hand, I only do one hour of German a week.

It's a tiring day. If I had the choice, I would start lessons later.

Pendant la récré

Usually, I talk with my friends and we eat lunch.

Normally, I stay outside and I play football, but sometimes I go to the canteen.

School Life

First Go:
..... /..... /.....

Où vas-tu à l'école?

la maternelle			technical college
	primary school	l'école publique *(f)*	
	secondary school		private school
	sixth form college	l'école confessionnelle *(f)*	

Je vais .... près de chez moi. .... parce que mes professeurs ont un bon sens de l'humour et ils sont très passionnants.
I go to the secondary school close to my home. I really like going there because my teachers have a .... and they are very ....

Mon école est .... J'y vais depuis l'âge de onze ans.
My school is a boarding school. I've been going there .... of eleven.

Je suis actuellement en seconde. Je vais aller .... l'année prochaine.
I'm currently in .... I'm going to go to technical college next year.

Décris ton école

Mon collège est ...	My school is very old...
...mais c'est génial .	...but it's great inside.
...mais c'est bien équipé.	...but it's .
...et sont mal équipés.	...and the school laboratories are .
L'ambiance à mon collège est très .	The at my school is very welcoming.
, il y a trois cents élèves.	In total, there are around three hundred .
Il y a un et même une piscine.	There is a modern sports hall and even a .

Second Go: ..... /..... /.....

School Life

Où vas-tu à l'école?

nursery school

primary school

secondary school

sixth form college

technical college

state school

private school

religious school

I go to the secondary school close to my home. I really like going there because my teachers have a good sense of humour and they are very engaging.

My school is a boarding school. I've been going there since the age of eleven.

I'm currently in year 11. I'm going to go to technical college next year.

Décris ton école

	My school is very old... ...but it's great inside. ...but it's well equipped. ...and the school laboratories are badly equipped.
	The atmosphere at my school is very welcoming.
	In total, there are around three hundred pupils.
	There is a modern sports hall and even a swimming pool.

School Pressures

First Go: ..... /..... /.....

Être sous pression

Il y a beaucoup de pression à l'école... ...pour obtenir de ______. ...pour être à la mode.	There's a lot of ______ at school... ...to get good marks. ...to be ______.
Je ne veux pas faire d' ______ ou échouer.	I don't want to make mistakes or ______.
J' ______ dur cette année donc j'espère... ... ______ mes examens. ...obtenir un bon bulletin scolaire. ...avoir de ______.	I studied ______ this year so I ______... ...to pass ______. ...to get a good ______. ...to have good results.
Je me sens sous forte pression... ...car j' ______ de devoir redoubler.	I feel ______... ...because I'm scared of having to ______.

'.............................. un examen' = 'to sit an exam'

Le règlement

D'un côté, ... aide à .... tous les élèves égaux.
On one hand, school uniform helps to make all pupils ....

De l'autre côté, il empêche les élèves d' ....
On the other hand, it .... students from being individuals.

Il ne faut pas être .... envers les professeurs ou .... dans les couloirs.
You mustn't be rude to the teachers or run ....

Il est .... de se maquiller.
It is forbidden to ....

Les incivilités sont ....
.... is unacceptable.

Si on ...., on sera en retenue.
If you break the school rules, you'll be ....

Il y a .... si on est en retard ou si on oublie ....
There are consequences if you're .... or if you forget your homework.

Second Go:
...... /...... /......

School Pressures

Être sous pression

	There's a lot of pressure at school... ...to get good marks. ...to be fashionable.
	I don't want to make mistakes or fail.
	I studied hard this year so I hope... ...to pass my exams. ...to get a good school report. ...to have good results.
	I feel under lots of pressure... ...because I'm scared of having to repeat the year.

................................., ... = 'to sit an exam'

Le règlement

On one hand, school uniform helps to make all pupils equal.

On the other hand, it prevents students from being individuals.

You mustn't be rude to the teachers or run in the corridors.

It is forbidden to wear make-up.

Rudeness is unacceptable.

If you break the school rules, you'll be in detention.

There are consequences if you're late or if you forget your homework.

Education Post-16

First Go: ..... /..... /.....

Après le collège

Après le collège, j'irai .... pour ....
After secondary school, I .... to sixth form college to do A-levels.

À l'avenir, je m'inscrirai
....
In the future, I .... to university.

Elle .... de faire
....
She intends to do an apprenticeship.

Je vais devenir .... afin d'être formé à ....
I'm going to become an apprentice to .... in construction.

J'ai vraiment hâte d'aller .... Mes frères sont ....
.... et .... et ils aiment beaucoup ça.
I .... to go to sixth form college. My brothers are in year 12 and year 13 and they really enjoy it.

Avant d'aller à l'université, j'ai envie de prendre ....
pour .... le monde et faire ....
Before going to university, ... take a gap year to discover the world and do some voluntary work.

Pourquoi continuer les études?

Il faut avoir une licence... ...pour faire mon ____________ .	You have to have a ____________ ... ...to do my preferred job.
____________ cherchent souvent... ...les gens qui ont le bac. ...les employés qualifiés.	Employers often ____________ ... ...people who have ____________ . ... ____________ .
Il y a plus de ____________ ... ...si on ____________ .	There are more job opportunities... ...if you continue studying.
Faire ____________ améliore mes chances de trouver un emploi... ...avec ____________ .	Doing an apprenticeship ____________ my chances of ____________ ... ...with a good salary.

Second Go: ...../...../.....	Education Post-16

Education Post-16

Après le collège

After secondary school, I will go to sixth form college to do A-levels.

In the future, I will apply to university.

She intends to do an apprenticeship.

I'm going to become an apprentice to be trained in construction.

I can't wait to go to sixth form college. My brothers are in year 12 and year 13 and they really enjoy it.

Before going to university, I want to take a gap year to discover the world and do some voluntary work.

Pourquoi continuer les études?

	You have to have a degree... ...to do my preferred job.
	Employers often look for... ...people who have A-levels. ...skilled employees.
	There are more job opportunities... ...if you continue studying.
	Doing an apprenticeship improves my chances of finding a job... ...with a good salary.

Career Choices and Ambitions

First Go: ..... /..... /.....

Le petit job

As-tu un ______ ?	Do you have a part-time job?
Je ______ le week-end... ...pour ______ de l'argent.	I babysit at the weekend... ...to earn money.
J'ai ______ dans un café,... ...cependant, je préférerais travailler dans ______.	I have a job in a café,... ...however, ______ to work in a hair salon.
Je ne suis pas ______,... ...mais je travaille dur. ...mais ______.	I'm not paid well,... ...but I ______. ...but I like working there.
Je m'entends bien avec ______.	I ______ with my boss.
Je viens d'aller à ______.	I've ______ to an interview.

Ton métier idéal

You don't need ' ' or ' ' when talking about what job you do.

Je veux être .... parce que je veux soigner ....
I want to be a nurse because I want to .... for sick people.

Je rêve d'être .... afin de .... l'injustice.
I .... of being a lawyer so that I can fight against injustice.

J'espère devenir .... comme ma mère.
I hope .... an engineer like my mum.

Je .... ce que je voudrais faire.
I don't know what I ....

Je .... avec un conseiller d'orientation.
I'm going to speak to ....

Je crois qu'être .... serait idéal pour moi car c'est .... enrichissant.
I believe that to be a vet .... for me because it's an .... job.

Pour moi, c'est important de .... de .... dans mon travail.
For me, it's important to find job satisfaction.

Second Go: ..... /..... /.....	**Career Choices and Ambitions**

Le petit job

	Do you have a part-time job?
	I babysit at the weekend... ...to earn money.
	I have a job in a café,... ...however, I would prefer to work in a hair salon.
	I'm not paid well,... ...but I work hard. ...but I like working there.
	I get on well with my boss.
	I've just been to an interview.

Ton métier idéal

You ______ need '____' or '____' when talking about what ______.

I want to be a nurse because I want to care for sick people.

I dream of being a lawyer so that I can fight against injustice.

I hope to become an engineer like my mum.

I don't know what I would like to do.

I'm going to speak to a careers advisor.

I believe that to be a vet would be ideal for me because it's an enriching job.

For me, it's important to find job satisfaction.

Mixed Practice Quizzes

Time for another round of quizzes — these tests cover the content on p.109-120. Tick the questions you get right and go back over any areas you find a bit tricky.

Quiz 1

Date: ...... / ...... / ......

1) Give two different words in French for 'a job'.
2) What is 'un bulletin scolaire' in English?
3) Translate into French: 'I had to drop IT to study art.'
4) What does 'sous forte pression' mean in English?
5) How do you say 'modern languages' in French?
6) Translate into French: 'I don't know what I would like to do after A-levels.'
7) What does this sentence mean in English?
   'Je vais aller au lycée près de chez moi l'année prochaine.'
8) What does 'en retenue' mean in English?
9) Translate into English: 'J'ai parlé avec un conseiller d'orientation.'
10) How do you say 'job opportunities' in French?

Total:

Quiz 2

Date: ...... / ...... / ......

1) Give an answer to this question in French: 'Comment vas-tu à l'école?'
2) How do you say 'the lessons are relaxed' in French?
3) Translate into English: 'Je vais être formé à la construction.'
4) In French, give a sentence to describe the atmosphere at your school.
5) Translate into French: 'I don't like working there.'
6) Give the French for: 'I talk with my friends during break.'
7) Translate into French:
   'My teacher has a good sense of humour and he is very engaging.'
8) What does this sentence mean in English?
   'Mes parents m'emmènent au collège en voiture.'
9) What is the French infinitive of the verb 'to prevent'?
10) Give the French for 'experiments'.

Total:

Mixed Practice Quizzes

Quiz 3

Date: ...... / ...... / ......

1) Translate into English: 'Elle est en seconde.'
2) What does this sentence mean in English? 'Au collège, il est interdit de courir dans les couloirs.'
3) What is 'un entretien' in English?
4) Explain why this sentence is incorrect: 'Je veux être un avocat.'
5) Give the French for: 'My friend has an artistic side.'
6) Translate into English: 'J'étudie dur parce que je veux avoir de bonnes notes.'
7) Give the English for 's'inscrire à la faculté'.
8) In French, give a reason why someone might want to continue with their studies.
9) Give three different types of school in French.
10) Translate into French: 'I stay outside with my friends during break.'

Total:

Quiz 4

Date: ...... / ...... / ......

1) What does this sentence mean in English? 'L'EPS ne sert à rien.'
2) Translate into French: 'I can't wait to do an apprenticeship.'
3) What does 'passer un examen' mean in English?
4) How do you say 'well equipped' and 'badly equipped' in French?
5) What does the French verb 'redoubler' mean in English?
6) Give the French for 'a term'.
7) Translate into English: 'Il ne faut pas enfreindre le règlement.'
8) What does this sentence mean in English? 'Mon frère rêve d'être médecin car il veut soigner les malades.'
9) Translate into French: 'We do three hours of Spanish a week.'
10) How do you say 'a good salary' in French?

Total:

Words for People and Objects

First Go: ..... /..... /.....

Masculine or feminine?

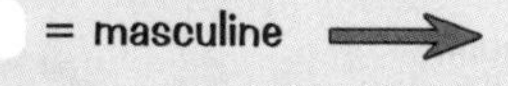

[ ] = masculine → .... livre intéressant *the interesting book*

[ ] = feminine → .... matière intéressante *the interesting subject*

[ ] word endings:

-age	-er	-isme
-ail	-et	-ment
-al	-ier	-oir
-eau	-in	-ou
-eil	-ing	

There are some exceptions.

[ ] word endings:

-aine	-ense	-ise
-ance	-esse	-sion
-anse	-ette	-té
-ée	-ie	-tion
-elle	-ière	-tude
-ence	-ine	-ure

Making nouns plural

Usually, add [ ] to make a noun [ ].

le chat *the cat* → .... *the cats*

Change 'le' or 'la' to [ ].

There are some [ ] plural forms:

Noun ending	Plural ending	Example	
-ail		le travail	
	-aux		les journaux
	-eaux		les bureaux
-eu		le jeu	
	-oux		les choux

A few nouns ending in [ ] add [ ], but most add [ ].

Nouns ending in [ ], [ ] or [ ] don't change in the [ ].

la souris *the mouse*  .... *the mice*

Second Go: ..... /..... /.....

Words for People and Objects

Masculine or feminine?

= → *the interesting book*

= → *the interesting subject*

word endings:

		-isme
-ail	-et	
-al		-oir
	-in	-ou
-eil	-ing	

There are ....

word endings:

-aine	-ense	
	-esse	-sion
-anse		-té
-ée	-ie	
		-tude
-ence	-ine	-ure

Making nouns plural

Usually, to make .

the cat → *the cats*

Change or to .

There are :

Noun ending	Plural ending	Example	
-ail		le travail	
-al		le journal	
-eau		le bureau	
-eu		le jeu	
-ou		le chou	

nouns ending in add , but most add .

Nouns ending don't .

the mouse → *the mice*

'The', 'A' and 'Some'

First Go: ..... / ..... / .....

'A'

= masculine

.... café *a coffee*

= feminine

.... tasse *a cup*

'The'

Masc. sing.	Fem. sing.
	la
Before vowels and sometimes 'h'	**Plural**
l'	

Using 'de' and 'à' with definite articles

'de' (/) and 'à' (/)
with 'le' and 'les' to form .

	le	la	l'	les
de +		de la	de l'	
à +	au			aux

Je vais .... parc d'attractions. *I'm going to the* ....

Je marche .... magasins. .... *to the shops.*

Je viens .... États-Unis. *I come from the* ....

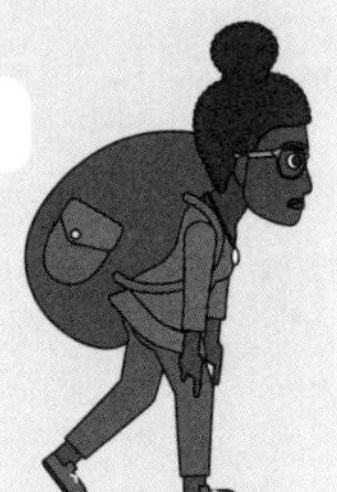

'Some' or 'any'

Use 'de' with a to say 'some' or 'any'.

Je voudrais .... soupe.
I .... *some soup.*

J'ai mangé .... gâteau.
I ate some ....

In sentences and after most ,
only use before the noun — you don't need an .

Je n'ai pas .... pain.
.... *any bread.*

J'ai .... fromage.
I have a bit of ....

Second Go: ..... /..... /.....

'The', 'A' and 'Some'

'A'

=

a coffee

=

a cup

'The'

Masc. sing.	Fem. sing.
Before vowels and sometimes 'h'	Plural

Using 'de' and 'à' with definite articles

'de' (/) and 'à' (/)
with to form .

	le	la	l'	les
de +				
à +				

I'm going to the theme park.

I'm walking to the shops.

I come from the United States.

'Some' or 'any'

Use with a to say 'some' or 'any'.

I would like some soup.

I ate some cake.

In and after ,
only use before — you don't need .

I don't have any bread.

I have a bit of cheese.

Words to Describe Things

First Go: ..... / ..... / .....

Adjectives 'agree'

Masculine singular — → le film .... *the funny film*

Masculine plural — → les films .... *the funny films*

Feminine singular — → la vache .... *the green cow*

Feminine plural — → les vaches .... *the green cows*

Some adjectives follow different rules...

Ending	Masc. sing.	Fem. sing.	Masc. pl.	Fem. pl.
	heureux		heureux	heureuses
-on, -en, -el, -il	bon	bonne		
-er			fiers	fières
		sportive	sportifs	
-c	blanc		blancs	

...and some are completely irregular

Before a masc. sing. noun starting with a vowel	Fem. sing.	Masc. pl.	Fem. pl.
vieil		vieux	
	belle	beaux	
nouvel			nouvelles
	folle		folles
long		longs	
tout			toutes
		rigolos	rigolotes

Second Go:
..... /..... /.....

Words to Describe Things

Adjectives 'agree'

Some adjectives follow different rules...

Ending	Masc. sing.	Fem. sing.	Masc. pl.	Fem. pl.
-x	heureux			
-on, -en, -el, -il	bon			
-er	fier			
-f	sportif			
-c	blanc			

...and some are completely irregular

Before a masc. sing. noun starting with a vowel	Fem. sing.	Masc. pl.	Fem. pl.
		vieux	
		beaux	
		nouveaux	
		fous	
		longs	
		tous	
		rigolos	

Words to Describe Things

First Go: ..... /..... /.....

Adjectives before the noun

Most adjectives go the noun, but these normally go the noun:

good *old* petit haut

mauvais *new* grand *false*

jeune *beautiful* *pretty* premier

Some adjectives change depending on if they're before or after .

ancien .... *(before)* / .... *(after)*

propre .... *(before)* / .... *(after)*

Possessive adjectives

	My	Your (inf. sing.)	His/ her/its	Our	Your (pl., form.)	Their
Masc. sing.		ton			votre	leur
Fem. sing.			sa	notre		leur
Pl.	mes		ses		vos	

These match the being :

Elle a trouvé .... stylo. *She found her* ....

'stylo' is .

Feminine nouns that take the article 'l'' use the .... possessive adjective.

'Some' and 'each'

= some

Add to make it plural.

J'ai acheté .... bonbons. *I bought some sweets.*

= each

never changes spelling.

Je lis .... nuit. *I read each night.*

'This' and 'these'

'Ce', and all mean 'this' — means 'these'.

Masc. sing.	Fem. sing.	Masc. words that take 'l''	Pl.
ce			

Second Go: ...../...../.....

Words to Describe Things

Adjectives before the noun

Most adjectives go ______, but these normally go ______:

good	old	small	high
bad	new	big	false
young	beautiful	pretty	first

Some adjectives change ______ depending on if they're ______ or ______ the noun.

former (before) / old (after)

own (before) / clean (after)

Possessive adjectives

	My	Your (inf. sing.)	His/ her/its	Our	Your (pl., form.)	Their
Masc. sing.						
Fem. sing.						
Pl.						

These match ______:

She found her pen.

'stylo' is ______.

Feminine nouns that take .... use the ....

'Some' and 'each'

______ = some

Add ______ to make it ______.

I bought some sweets.

______ = each

______ never ______.

I read each night.

'This' and 'these'

______, ______ and ______ all mean 'this' — ______ means 'these'.

Masc. sing.	Fem. sing.	Masc. words that take 'l''	Pl.

Words to Compare Things

First Go: ...... / ...... / ......

Comparatives and superlatives

______ ... ______ ... *more ... than ...* → Salma est .... bizarre .... moi.
Salma is weirder than me.

le plus ... ______ ... → Paul est le plus bizarre.
Paul is ....

moins ... que ... ______ ... ______ ... → Il est moins fort que moi.
He is .... strong .... me.

______ ... *the least ...* → Il est .... fort.
He is the least strong.

aussi ... que ... ______ ... ______ ... → Elle est aussi grande que moi.
She is ...... tall ...... me.

Agreement

Comparative and ______ adjectives ______ with the word they ______ . → Elle est plus ....
She is more sporty.

If you're saying 'the most' and 'the least', 'the' also needs to ______ . → Ils sont .... plus jeunes.
They are the youngest.

Exceptions

You don't use ______ or ______ with these words:

Adjective	Comparative	Superlative
______ good	**meilleur(e)(s)** ______	**le/la/les meilleur(e)(s)** ______
mauvais(e)(s) ______	______ worse	______ the worst

Second Go: ..... /..... /.....

Words to Compare Things

Comparatives and superlatives

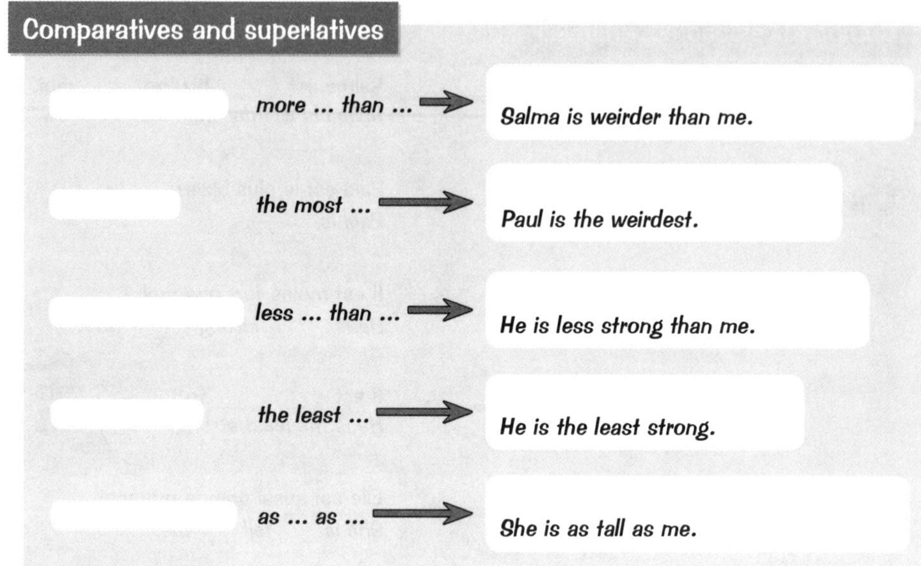

Agreement

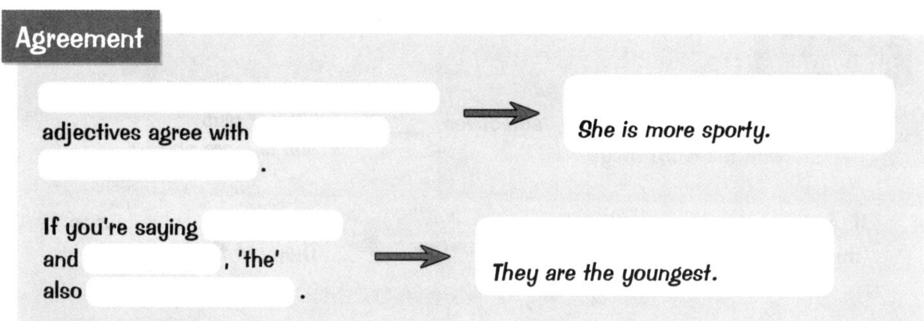

Exceptions

You don't use with :

Adjective	Comparative	Superlative
good		
bad		

Words to Describe Actions

First Go: ..... /..... /.....

Adverbs

Take the ______ form of the adjective and add ______.

adroit *skilful* → .... → .... *skilfully*

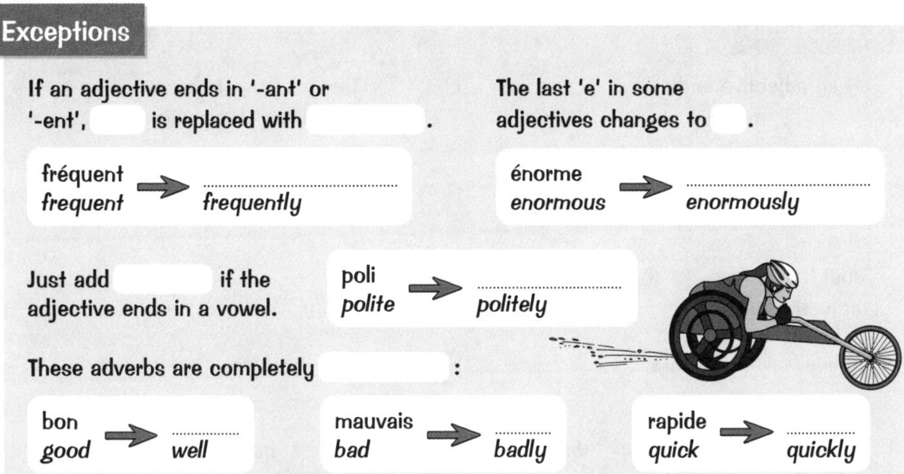

Exceptions

If an adjective ends in '-ant' or '-ent', ______ is replaced with ______.

fréquent *frequent* → .... *frequently*

The last 'e' in some adjectives changes to ______.

énorme *enormous* → .... *enormously*

Just add ______ if the adjective ends in a vowel.

poli *polite* → .... *politely*

These adverbs are completely ______:

bon *good* → .... *well*

mauvais *bad* → .... *badly*

rapide *quick* → .... *quickly*

Useful adverbs and adverbial phrases

These adverbs describe ______ or ______ something happens:

tous les jours	______	tôt	______	récemment	______
______	*sometimes*	tard	______	______	*soon*
immédiatement	______	______	*before*	aujourd'hui	______
en même temps	______	______	*already*	______	*tomorrow*

These adverbs describe ______ something happens:

______	*here*	______	*near*
là	______	loin	______
______	*everywhere*		
quelque part	______		

These adverbial phrases often go at the ______ of ______:

par conséquent	______
en tout cas	______
______	*absolutely*
par hasard	______
______	*anyway*

Second Go: ..... / ..... / .....

Words to Describe Actions

Adverbs

Take the ______ of ______ and ______.

skilful → ______ → *skilfully*

Exceptions

If an adjective ends in ______ or ______, '-nt' is ______ with ______.

frequent → *frequently*

The ______ in some adjectives changes to ______.

enormous → *enormously*

Just ______ if the adjective ends in a ______.

polite → *politely*

These ______ are ______:

good → *well*

bad → *badly*

quick → *quickly*

Useful adverbs and adverbial phrases

These adverbs describe ______:

______	*every day*	______	*early*	______	*recently*
______	*sometimes*	______	*late*	______	*soon*
______	*immediately*	______	*before*	______	*today*
______	*at the same time*	______	*already*	______	*tomorrow*

These adverbs describe ______:

______	*here*	______	*near*
______	*there*	______	*far*

______ *everywhere*

______ *somewhere*

These ______ phrases often go ______:

______ *consequently*

______ *anyway*

______ *absolutely*

______ *by chance*

______ *anyway*

Words to Compare Actions

First Go: ..... /..... /.....

Comparative adverbs

... ... more ... than ... → Jean lit .... vite .... Souad.
Jean reads more quickly than Souad.

moins ... que ... ... → Souad lit moins souvent que Danielle.
Souad reads .... Danielle.

aussi ... que ... ... → Danielle lit aussi vite que Jacques.
Danielle reads .... Jacques.

... *as much as* ... → Danielle lit .... Jacques.
Danielle reads as much as Jacques.

'The most'

Use .... to say 'the most...'.

Ils conduisent .... dangereusement.
They drive the most dangerously.

Vivienne chante .... musicalement.
Vivienne sings the most musically.

Always use .... — never 'la' or 'les'.

Exceptions

Adverb	Comparative	Superlative
well	**mieux**	**le mieux**
mal	worse	the worst
beaucoup	more	the most
little	**moins**	**le moins**

Je joue au foot mieux que Ben.
I play football .... than Ben.

Sandrine travaille ....
Sandrine works the most.

Je te vois le moins souvent.
I see you .... often.

Second Go: ..... / ..... / .....

Words to Compare Actions

Comparative adverbs

more ... than ... → Jean reads more quickly than Souad.

less ... than ... → Souad reads less often than Danielle.

as ... as ... → Danielle reads as fast as Jacques.

as much as ... → Danielle reads as much as Jacques.

'The most'

Use to say .

They drive the most dangerously.

Vivienne sings the most musically.

Exceptions

Adverb	Comparative	Superlative
well		
badly		
lots		
little		

I play football better than Ben.

Sandrine works the most.

I see you the least often.

Words to Say How Much

First Go: ..... / ..... / .....

Intensifiers

Intensifiers add ______ to adjectives and ______.

Camille est trop sérieuse.
Camille is .... serious.

La géographie est .... intéressante.
Geography is not very interesting.

J'écris très vite.
I write ....

Ils courent .... lentement.
They run quite slowly.

Intensifiers always go .... the adjective or ....

Quantifiers

Quantifiers show ______ there is of something.

trop de ______ / ______ ______ *a little (bit of)*
______ *lots of / many* assez de ______

Nous avons .... argent.
We have little money.

J'ai assez de chaussures.
I have .... shoes.

Use ______ if the noun starts with ______.

Adverbs can be intensifiers

particulièrement ______ ______ *enormously*
______ *really* exceptionnellement ______
incroyablement ______

Ce film est .... passionnant.
This film is really exciting.

La montagne est incroyablement haut<u>e</u>. *The mountain is .... high.*

The ______ still needs to ______.

Second Go: ..... /..... /.....

Words to Say How Much

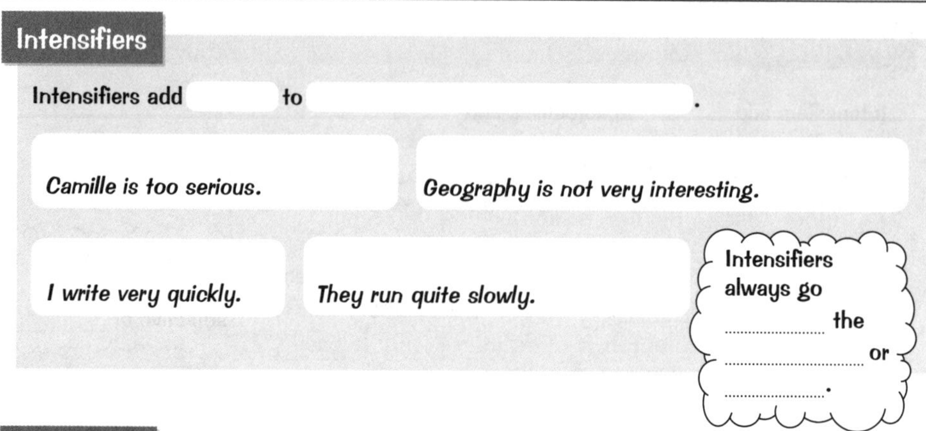

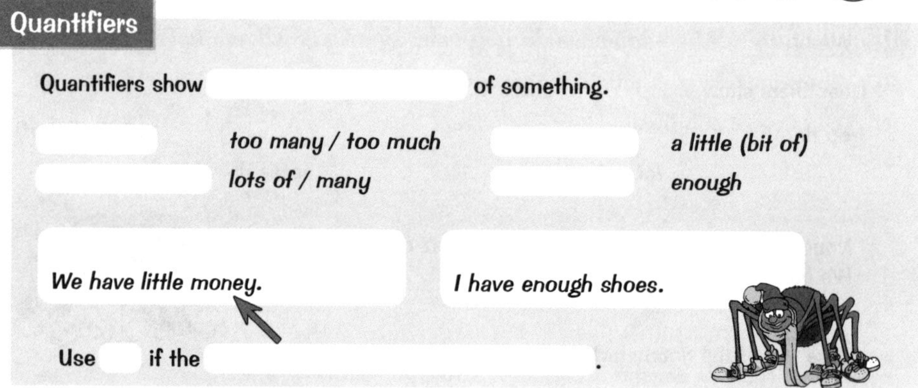

Mixed Practice Quizzes

It's time for a batch of quizzes on the nuts and bolts of French — grammar (try to stay calm). All the questions are based on the content on p.123-138.

Quiz 1

Date: ...... / ...... / ......

1) How do you change most adjectives to agree with feminine plural nouns?
2) True or false? 'His car' is 'son voiture' in French.
3) Translate into French: 'I speak to Henri every day.'
4) Complete the following sentence: 'De' and 'les' combine to form '...'.
5) What are the plural forms of 'le travail' and 'le cheval'?
6) Translate into French: 'We have enough money.'
7) Give the comparative and superlative forms of the adjective 'mauvais'.
8) Which form of an adjective do you use to make an adverb in French?
9) What does 'le plus jeune' mean in English?
10) Give five of the feminine word endings.

Total:

Quiz 2

Date: ...... / ...... / ......

1) What does 'quelque' mean in English? Does it change in the plural?
2) Which type of word does an intensifier go before in a sentence?
3) Give the comparative and superlative forms of the adverb 'bien'.
4) True or false? 'Politely' in French is 'poliement'.
5) Give all the different forms of the French adjective 'sportif'.
6) Translate into French: 'I would like some cake and some water.'
7) Which adjective in the following list doesn't go before the noun? 'mauvais', 'joli', 'vieux', 'long', 'jeune', 'haut', 'bon'.
8) Translate into French: 'I don't have any soup.'
9) What does 'autant que' mean in English?
10) What does the adverbial phrase 'par hasard' mean in English?

Total:

Mixed Practice Quizzes

Quiz 3

Date: ...... / ...... / ......

1) Give all the different forms of the French adjective 'fou'.
2) True or false? Nouns ending in '-s', '-x' and '-z' don't change spelling in the plural form.
3) Translate into French: 'I'm as tall as my father, but I'm shorter than my sister.'
4) Translate into English: 'Tu manges trop de bonbons et peu de légumes.'
5) Complete the following sentence: 'À' and 'les' combine to form '...'.
6) Give all the different forms of the possessive adjective 'our' in French.
7) Turn the adjective 'fréquent' into an adverb.
8) Give two examples of adverbs that can be used as intensifiers.
9) Complete the following sentence with the correct word: 'Nous chantons ... plus musicalement.'
10) Give all the different forms of the French adjective 'rigolo'.

Total:

Quiz 4

Date: ...... / ...... / ......

1) Give five of the masculine word endings.
2) Translate into English: 'Elle est plus vieille que lui.'
3) What are the comparative and superlative forms of the adjective 'bon'?
4) True or false? All nouns ending in '-ou' add '-x' in the plural form.
5) Complete this sentence with the correct form of 'this' and then translate it into English: 'Je préférerais acheter ... ordinateur.'
6) Give four French adverbs that describe when or how often something happens.
7) Translate into French: 'She runs too slowly.'
8) Give the comparative and superlative forms of the adverb 'mal'.
9) Give all the different forms of the French adjective 'premier'.
10) Translate into French: 'He sees her more often than me.'

Total:

I, Me, You, We, Them

First Go: ..... /..... /.....

Subject pronouns

I	
You (inf. sing.)	tu
He/she/it/one/we	
We	nous
You (pl., form.)	
They	

Subject pronouns replace the person or thing .

.... est musicien.
.... est fana de musique classique.
My brother is a musician.
He is a fan of classical music.

Direct object pronouns

Me	You (inf. sing.)	Him/her/it	Us	You (pl., form.)	Them
me			nous		

Direct object pronouns replace the thing .

.... voit son amie.
He sees his friend.
→
.... voit.
He sees her.

'le' and 'la' become if followed by a vowel.

J'ai regardé ....
I watched the film.
→
Je ...... ai regardé.
I watched it.

Indirect object pronouns

Me	You (inf. sing.)	Him/her/it	Us	You (pl., form.)	Them
me			nous		

Indirect objects are things that are the action, but not .

.... donne le cadeau à son amie.
He gives .... to his friend.
→
.... donne le cadeau.
He gives her ....

Second Go:
..... / ..... / .....

I, Me, You, We, Them

Subject pronouns

I	
You (inf. sing.)	
He/she/it/one/we	
We	
You (pl., form.)	
They	

Subject pronouns ______ the ______ doing ______.

My brother is a musician.
He is a fan of classical music.

Direct object pronouns

Me	You (inf. sing.)	Him/ her/it	Us	You (pl., form.)	Them

Direct object pronouns ______ the ______.

He sees his friend. → *He sees her.*

I watched the film. → *I watched it.*

______ and ______ become ______ if followed by ______.

Indirect object pronouns

Me	You (inf. sing.)	Him/ her/it	Us	You (pl., form.)	Them

Indirect objects are things that are ______.

He gives the present to his friend.

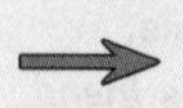

He gives her the present.

Something, There, Any

First Go: ..... /..... /.....

Indefinite pronouns

Use indefinite pronouns to talk about ______ and ______ things.

quelqu'un	______	______	*several*
tout le monde	______	______	*all / everything*
______	*something*	chacun(e)	______

Tout le monde aime le chocolat. .... *likes chocolate.*

'Y'

'Y' means ______ when it replaces a location.

Elle va à la banque.
She's .... *to* ....

→ Elle y va.
She's ....

It's used in these ______ :

....
Let's do it! / Let's go!

Vas-y!
.... ! / .... !

Il y a...
.... / ....

With a verb that uses ______ , 'y' can replace the noun — it means ______ or ______ .

Je pense ...... l'idée.
I'm thinking about the idea.

→ J'y pense.
I'm thinking ....

'En'

'En' = ______ , 'of them', ______ or 'any'.

.... des oranges?
Do you have any oranges?

→ Oui, j'en ai.
Yes, I have ....

Non, je .... pas.
No, I don't have any.

.... des abeilles?
Are you scared of bees?

→ Oui, ... peur.
Yes, I'm scared of them.

With a verb that uses ______ , 'en' can replace the ______ .

Tu as besoin ....
You need help.

→ Tu .... besoin.
You need it.

Second Go:
..... /..... /.....

Something, There, Any

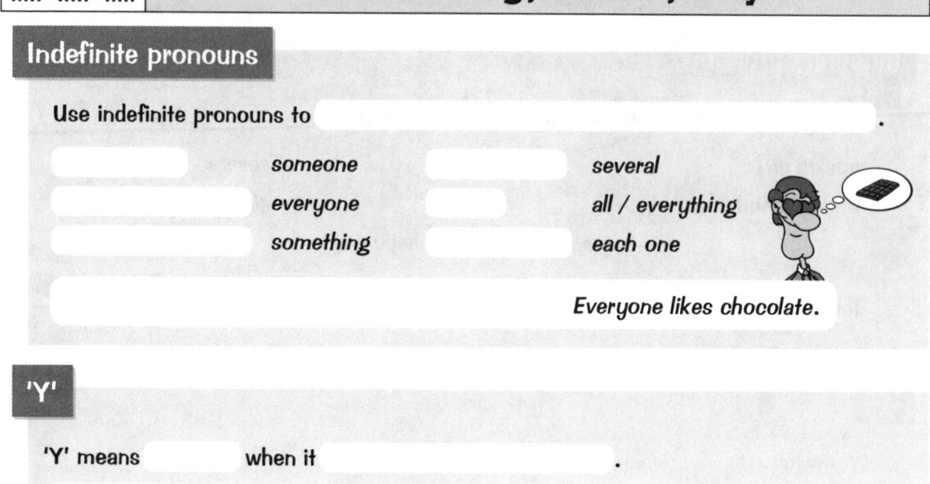

Indefinite pronouns

Use indefinite pronouns to .

someone
everyone
something
several
all / everything
each one

Everyone likes chocolate.

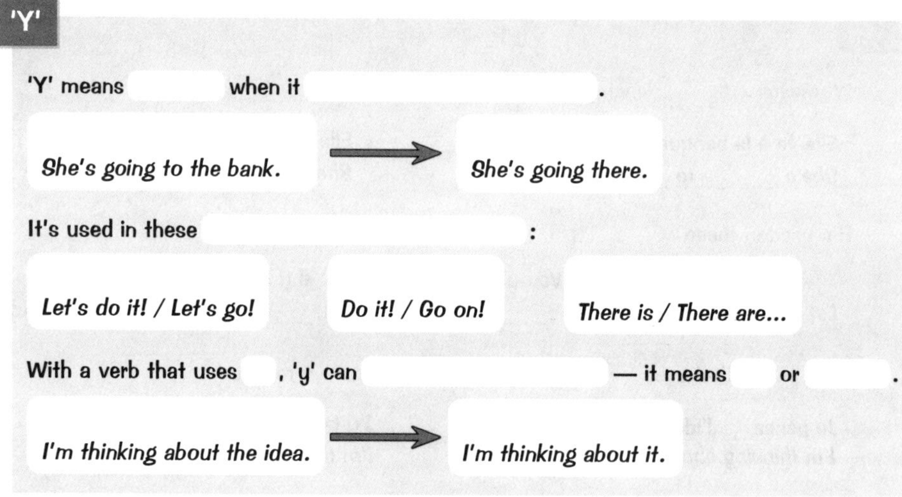

'Y'

'Y' means when it .

She's going to the bank. → *She's going there.*

It's used in these :

Let's do it! / Let's go!
Do it! / Go on!
There is / There are...

With a verb that uses , 'y' can — it means or .

I'm thinking about the idea. → *I'm thinking about it.*

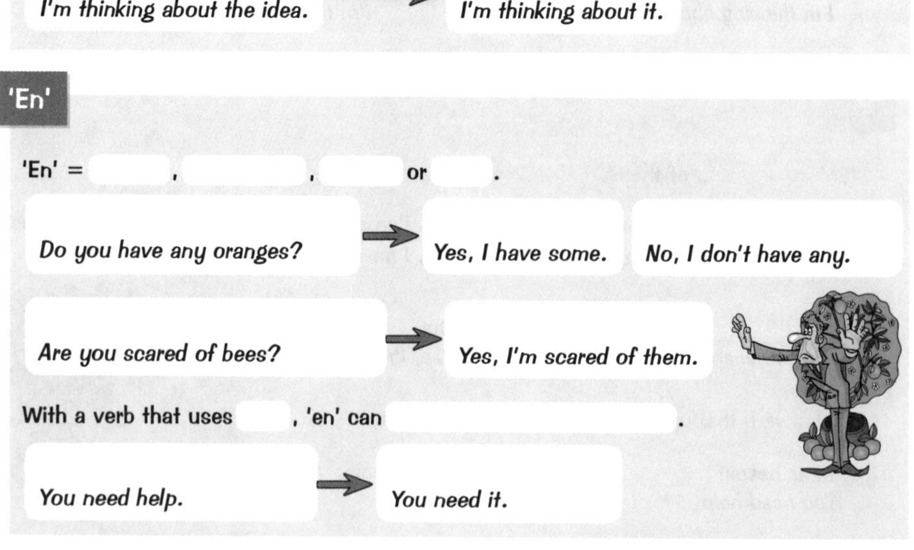

'En'

'En' = , , or .

Do you have any oranges? → *Yes, I have some.* *No, I don't have any.*

Are you scared of bees? → *Yes, I'm scared of them.*

With a verb that uses , 'en' can .

You need help. → *You need it.*

Object and Emphatic Pronouns

First Go: ..... /..... /.....

Order of object pronouns

Pronouns follow this order if there's more ______ them:

ne	me ______ se nous ______	______ la les	______ leur	y	______	verb	pas

Elle .... donne.
She gives it to me.

Il .... aura beaucoup.
There will be a lot of them.

Nous ne les aimons pas.
We .....

If you use 'avoir' or 'être' with a main verb, the pronouns go ______ verbs.

Elle .... donné.
She gave it to me.

If you use a verb with an infinitive, the object pronouns go ______ verbs.

Je peux ....
I can give it to her.

Emphatic pronouns

Me		Us	nous
You (inf. sing.)	toi	You (pl., form.)	
Him/her/one		Them	

There are four ways to use emphatic pronouns:

1. On their own, or after ______ :

   Qui parle? ....! ....!
   Who's speaking? Me! It's me!

2. To ______ things:

   Il est plus petit que toi.
   He's ....

3. To give ______ :

   Écoutez-nous!
   ....!

4. After ______ :

   Je suis allé ....
   I went with them.

Add ______ to the end of an emphatic pronoun to say ______ .

Il le fait ....
He does it himself.

Elles l'ont écrit ....
They wrote it themselves.

Second Go:
..... /..... /.....

Object and Emphatic Pronouns

Order of object pronouns

Pronouns if there's of them:

	me	le			

She gives it to me.

There will be a lot of them.

We don't like them.

If you use or with a main verb, the pronouns go .

She gave it to me.

If you use a verb with an , the go .

I can give it to her.

Emphatic pronouns

Me		Us	
You (inf. sing.)		You (pl., form.)	
Him/her/one		Them	

There are four ways to use emphatic pronouns:

1. On , or :

Who's speaking? Me! It's me!

2. To :

He's smaller than you.

3. To :

Listen to us!

4. After :

I went with them.

Add to an emphatic pronoun to .

He does it himself.

They wrote it themselves.

Relative and Interrogative Pronouns

First Go: ..... /..... /.....

Relative pronouns

Relative pronouns introduce .... to a sentence.

'Qui' is used for the .... of the sentence:

> Le bébé qui a volé les ballons.
> *The baby .... stole the balloons.*

'Que' is used for the .... of the sentence:

> Les ballons que le bébé a volés.
> *The balloons .... the baby stole.*

Dont

'Dont' has three main meanings:

1. 'about ....':

> L'araignée dont on a parlé.
> *The spider .... we talked.*

2. '............':

> La chef dont le fils est maçon.
> *The chef .... son is a builder.*

3. 'of ....':

> J'ai six films dont un est une comédie.
> *I've got six films, ... one is a comedy.*

Interrogative pronouns

You can use 'qui' (............) and 'que' (............) to ask questions...

...as the .... of a question:

> Qui parle?
> *............ is speaking?*

> Qu'est-ce qui se passe?
> *............ is happening?*

'............' changes to 'qu'est-ce qui' when it's the ....

...as the .... of the question:

> Qui connaissez-vous?
> *............ do you know?*

> Que savez-vous?
> *............ do you know?*

...after .... :

> Tu parles avec qui?
> *............ are you talking to?*

> De quoi parles-tu?
> *............ are you talking about?*

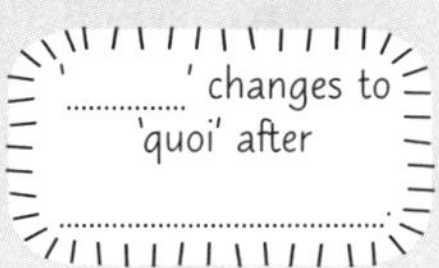

Second Go:
..... /..... /.....

Relative and Interrogative Pronouns

Relative pronouns

Relative pronouns to a sentence.

is used for of the sentence:

The baby who stole the balloons.

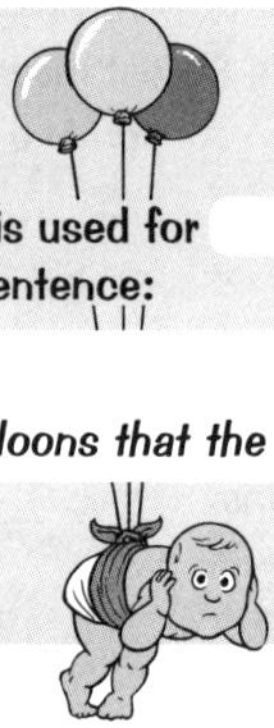

is used for of the sentence:

The balloons that the baby stole.

Dont

'Dont' has three main meanings:

1 ' ':

L'araignée dont on a parlé.

2 ' ':

La chef dont le fils est maçon.

3 ' ':

J'ai six films dont un est une comédie.

Interrogative pronouns

You can use ('who') and ('what') to ...

...as the of a :

Who is speaking?

What is happening?

'Que' changes to .... when it's the ....

...as the of the :

Who do you know?

What do you know?

...after :

Who are you talking to?

What are you talking about?

'Que' changes to .... after ....

Possessive and Demonstrative Pronouns

First Go: ..... /..... /.....

Possessive pronouns

Possessive pronouns replace a noun that ______ to someone.

They need to ______ :

	Mine	Yours (inf. sing.)	His/her/ its	Ours	Yours (pl., form)	Theirs
Masc. sing.	le mien		le sien	le nôtre		le leur
Fem. sing.		la tienne		la nôtre	la vôtre	la leur
Pl. (m/f)	les miens/ miennes	les tiens/ tiennes	les siens/ siennes		les vôtres	

Le .... est ici. C'est le mien.
The red hat is here. It's ....

Ces ....? Ce sont les nôtres.
These books? They're ....

Celui, celle, ceux, celles

These demonstrative pronouns mean 'this one', ______, ______ or 'the one(s)':

Masc. sing.	celui
Fem. sing.	celle
Masc. pl.	ceux
Fem. pl.	celles

J'aime ce gâteau, mais celui qu'on a mangé hier ....
I like ...., but .... we ate yesterday was better.

Ceci, cela, ça

These demonstrative pronouns mean ______ or ______ :

Ceci est ....
.... is interesting.

Cela ....!
.... isn't true!

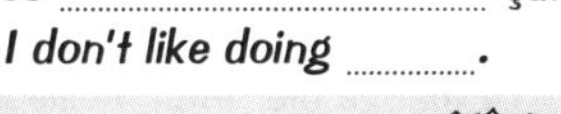

Je .... ça.
I don't like doing ....

.... J'aime celui-ci, mais celui-là ....
There are two cakes. I like ...., but .... is better.

Add '-ci' to mean ______ . Add '-là' to mean ______ .

Second Go: ..... /..... /.....

Possessive and Demonstrative Pronouns

Possessive pronouns

Possessive pronouns ________ a ______ that ________ to someone.

They need to ______ :

	Mine	Yours (inf. sing.)	His/her/its	Ours	Yours (pl., form)	Theirs
Masc. sing.	le mien		le sien	le nôtre	le vôtre	
Fem. sing.		la tienne	la sienne		la vôtre	la leur
Pl. (m/f)	les miens/ miennes	les tiens/ tiennes		les nôtres		les leurs

Le chapeau rouge est ici. C'est le mien.

Ces livres? Ce sont les nôtres.

Celui, celle, ceux, celles

These demonstrative pronouns mean ________ , ________ , ______ or ________ :

Masc. sing.	celui
Fem. sing.	celle
Masc. pl.	ceux
Fem. pl.	celles

J'aime ce gâteau, mais celui qu'on a mangé hier était meilleur.

Ceci, cela, ça

These demonstrative pronouns mean ______ or ______ :

Ceci est intéressant.

Cela n'est pas vrai!

Je n'aime pas faire ça.

Il y a deux gâteaux. J'aime celui-ci, mais celui-là est meilleur.

Add '-ci' to mean ____________ . Add '-là' to mean ____________ .

Joining Words

First Go: ..... /..... /.....

Conjunctions for linking sentences

	but	ou bien		ainsi	/
et			*then*	ensuite	/
ou			*therefore / so*	...	*neither...nor*

These conjunctions sentences :

J'ai un petit job... ... je mets de l'argent de côté chaque mois.	I have a ... ...therefore I every month.
Les fleurs sont ... ...et l'herbe est verte.	The flowers are light blue... ... the is green.

Use 'ou' to give .

Amélie .... infirmière ou ingénieure.
Amélie wants to be a nurse .... an engineer.

'ou' = '............'
'où' = '........................'

Conjunctions for adding information

	because		*while*
puisque		par contre	
quand			*when / as soon as*
	however		*for example*
	like	y compris	
si		même si	

These conjunctions add to a sentence,
e.g. a , a contradiction or a :

Je déteste le tabac... ... c'est mauvais pour la santé.	I hate ... ...because it's bad for .
Même s'ils sont délicieux,...	they're delicious,... ...I don't want them.

Second Go:
..... /..... /.....

Joining Words

Conjunctions for linking sentences

but	*or else*	*therefore / so*
and	*then*	*then / next*
or	*therefore / so*	*neither...nor*

These conjunctions :

	I have a part-time job... ...therefore I save some money every month.
	The flowers are light blue... ...and the grass is green.

Use to give .

Amélie wants to be a nurse or an engineer.

'..........' = 'or'
'..........' = 'where'

Conjunctions for adding information

because	*while*
since	*on the other hand*
when	*when / as soon as*
however	*for example*
like	*including*
if	*even if*

These conjunctions add to a sentence,
e.g. a , a or a :

	I hate smoking... ...because it's bad for your health.
	Even if they're delicious,... ...I don't want them.

Prepositions

First Go: ..... / ..... / .....

À

'À' can mean ______, 'in' or ______.

Elle ...... à Lyon. *She's going ...... Lyon.*

Je suis à la .... *I'm ...... home.*

Some ______ are followed by 'à' when they go ______ a noun.

Je joue aux échecs. *I ....*

De

'De' can mean ______ or ______.

une tasse de thé *a ....*

Jean vient du Canada.
Jean ....

Some ______ are followed by 'de' when they go ______ a noun.

Il s'agit d'un problème.
It's ....

En

'En' can mean ______ or ______.

Je vais en Iran en mai.
I'm going ....

Use it to say ______ something ______.

Il a lu l'article en cinq minutes.
He read the article ....

It describes what something's ______.

une veste en cuir *a ....*

Prepositions of time

avant ______
après ______
______ *for*
______ *since / for*
jusqu'à ______
______ *during / for*

Elle ...... aller ...... une semaine.
She is going to go there for a ....

J'y ai travaillé .... un mois.
I worked there for a ....

Prepositions of position

______ *on*
______ *under*
dans ______
derrière ______
______ *in front of*
à côté de ______

Mon .... est dans ma ....
My passport is ...... my suitcase.

Other prepositions

______ *with*
______ *without*
à cause de ______
______ *instead of*
chez ______
grâce à ______

Second Go: ..... / ..... / .....

Prepositions

À

'À' can mean ______, ______ or ______.

She's going to Lyon.

I'm at home.

Some ______ are ______ 'à' when they go ______ a ______.

I play chess.

De

'De' can mean ______ or ______.

a cup of tea

Jean comes from Canada.

Some ______ are ______ by ______ when they go ______ a ______.

It's about a problem.

En

'En' can mean ______ or ______.

I'm going to Iran in May.

Use it to say ______ something ______.

He read the article in five minutes.

It describes what ______.

a leather jacket

Prepositions of time

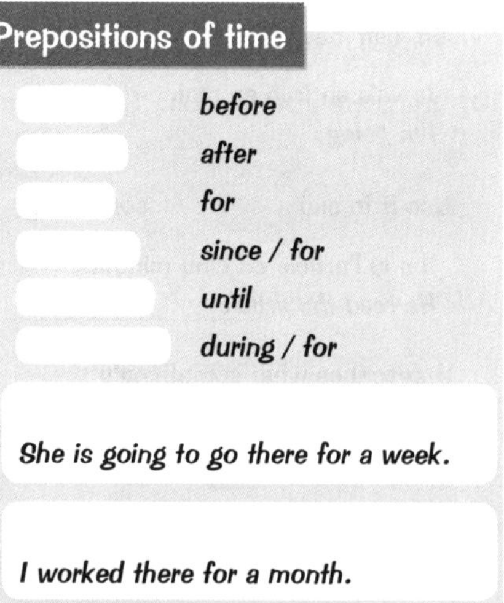

______ before

______ after

______ for

______ since / for

______ until

______ during / for

She is going to go there for a week.

I worked there for a month.

Prepositions of position

______ on

______ under

______ in

______ behind

______ in front of

______ next to

My passport is in my suitcase.

Other prepositions

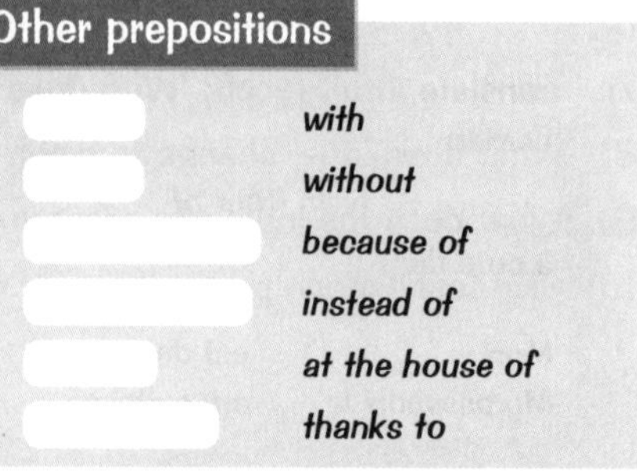

______ with

______ without

______ because of

______ instead of

______ at the house of

______ thanks to

Mixed Practice Quizzes

Pronouns, prepositions and things that don't begin with 'p' — these quizzes cover p.141-154. Do the quizzes one at a time and make sure you check your answers.

Quiz 1

Date: ...... / ...... / ......

1) Give four French conjunctions used for adding information to a sentence.
2) Translate into French: 'I can give it to them.'
3) Give two ways you can use emphatic pronouns in French.
4) What does the preposition 'à côté de' mean in English?
5) Complete the list of French direct object pronouns: 'me', 'te'...
6) Translate into English: 'J'aime cette araignée, mais celle-là est plus belle.'
7) True or false? When it's a relative pronoun, 'qui' is used for the object of the sentence.
8) What does 'le tien' mean in English?
9) Give three ways that the pronoun 'en' can be translated into English.
10) Translate into French: 'She is going to Paris in November.'

Total:

Quiz 2

Date: ...... / ...... / ......

1) Give the three main meanings of 'dont'.
2) What does 'y' mean in English when it replaces a location in a sentence?
3) Translate into English: 'Ce sont les vôtres.'
4) If the pronouns 'te' and 'le' are used in the same sentence, which one should come first?
5) What do the conjunctions 'puisque' and 'lorsque' mean in English?
6) Give two ways the subject pronoun 'on' can be translated into English.
7) Translate into French: 'Who does she know?'
8) What does 'que' change to when it's used after a preposition?
9) What does the indefinite pronoun 'tout le monde' mean in English?
10) Give four French prepositions of time.

Total:

Mixed Practice Quizzes

Quiz 3

Date: ...... / ...... / ......

1) Translate into French: 'She is thinking about it.'
2) Give five French conjunctions used to link sentences together.
3) Translate into English: 'Nous l'avons écrit nous-mêmes.'
4) Complete the list of French subject pronouns: 'je', 'tu'...
5) Which French preposition is used to say what something is made of?
6) What do the pronouns 'ceci', 'cela' and 'ça' mean in English?
7) Give two French pronouns you can use to ask questions.
8) Give three things that the preposition 'à' can mean in English.
9) Translate into English: 'Ils nous donnent le gâteau.'
10) Complete the list of French emphatic pronouns: 'moi', 'toi'...

Total:

Quiz 4

Date: ...... / ...... / ......

1) What are the French words for 'something' and 'someone'?
2) True or false? You add '-même' to the end of an emphatic pronoun to mean 'mine'.
3) Translate into English: 'J'ai quatre cadeaux dont un est une veste.'
4) Which subject pronoun would you use to replace 'mes sœurs'?
5) Translate into English: 'Le maçon qui a trouvé les abeilles.'
6) Give the French prepositions for 'under', 'on' and 'behind'.
7) Translate into French: 'There are a lot of them.'
8) What does the conjunction 'y compris' mean in English?
9) Complete the list of French indirect object pronouns: 'me', 'te'...
10) Which French preposition means 'at the house of?'

Total:

Verbs in the Present Tense

First Go: ..... / ..... / .....

The present tense

The present tense describes something that's __________ .

Je mange une pomme.
I .... an apple. / I ...... an apple.

Ils .... du lait.
They are drinking milk. / They drink milk.

It also describes something that happens ______ .

............, je fais du jogging. *On Mondays, I ....*

To find the stem of regular verbs, take the ______ ,
then ______ the final ____ letters.

regarder *to watch* → ....

finir *to finish* → ......

vendre *to sell* → ....

Then add an ______ to the ______ to show ______ the action.

'-er' endings

je	
tu	-es
il/elle/on	-e
nous	
vous	-ez
ils/elles	

je ....
I watch

nous ....
we watch

elles ....
they watch

'-ir' endings

je	
tu	-is
il/elle/on	
nous	
vous	
ils/elles	-issent

tu ....
you finish

il ....
he finishes

vous ....
you finish

'-re' endings

je	
tu	
il/elle/on	
nous	-ons
vous	-ez
ils/elles	

je ....
I sell

elle ....
she sells

ils ....
they sell

Second Go: ...../...../.....

Verbs in the Present Tense

The present tense

The present tense describes ______.

I am eating an apple. / I eat an apple.

They are drinking milk. / They drink milk.

It also describes something that ______.

On Mondays, I go jogging.

To find the stem of ______ verbs, take ______, then ______.

to watch →

to finish →

to sell →

Then add ______ to ______ to show ______.

'-er' endings

je	
tu	
il/elle/on	
nous	
vous	
ils/elles	

I watch

we watch

they watch

'-ir' endings

je	
tu	
il/elle/on	
nous	
vous	
ils/elles	

you finish

he finishes

you finish

'-re' endings

je	
tu	
il/elle/on	
nous	
vous	
ils/elles	

I sell

she sells

they sell

Irregular Verbs in the Present Tense

First Go: ..... /..... /.....

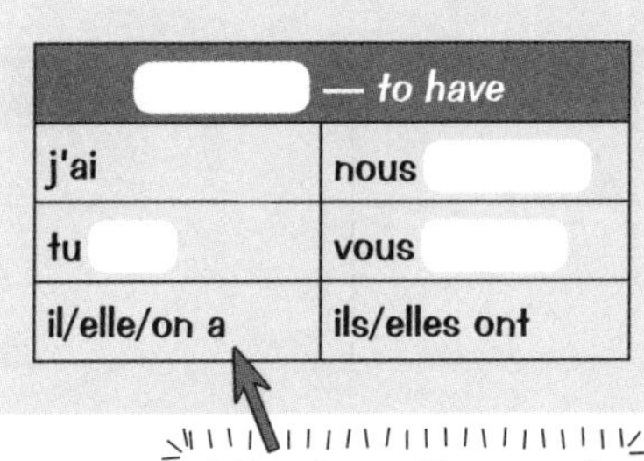

______ — to have	
j'ai	nous ______
tu ______	vous ______
il/elle/on a	ils/elles ont

'a' is a form of '............'.
'à' is a ....

être — ______	
je ______	nous sommes
tu es	vous ______
il/elle/on ______	ils/elles sont

______ — to make / do	
je ______	nous faisons
tu ______	vous ______
il/elle/on fait	ils/elles ______

______ — to go	
je ______	nous ______
tu vas	vous ______
il/elle/on ______	ils/elles vont

'Devoir' is a ....
'Les devoirs' = '.....................'

devoir — ______ / ______	
je dois	nous ______
tu ______	vous ______
il/elle/on doit	ils/elles doivent

'Savoir' = 'to know ....'
'Connaître' = 'to know .... or a ....'

______ — to know	
je ______	nous ______
tu ______	vous savez
il/elle/on sait	ils/elles ______

______ — to be able to / can	
je ______	nous ______
tu peux	vous ______
il/elle/on ______	ils/elles peuvent

vouloir — ______	
je ______	nous voulons
tu ______	vous ______
il/elle/on ______	ils/elles veulent

Second Go:
...../...../.....

Irregular Verbs in the Present Tense

— to have	

'......' is a form of 'avoir'.
'......' is a preposition.

— to be	

— to make / do	

— to go	

'......................' is a verb.
'..............................' = 'homework'

— must / to have to	

'......................' = 'to know something'
'..............................' = 'to know someone or a place'

— to know	

— to be able to / can	

— to want	

More About the Present Tense

First Go: ..... /..... /.....

Infinitives

When two verbs are used together, the ______ verb stays in the ______.

Je veux .... les autres. *I want to help ....*.

Not all verbs can be followed directly by an infinitive — some need a ______.

These verbs need ____ before an infinitive:

______ *to begin*
______ *to learn*
______ *to succeed*
______ *to succeed in / to manage*

Elle .... écouter.
She starts listening.

These verbs need ____ before an infinitive:

______ *to try*
______ *to decide*
______ *to stop (oneself)*
______ *to threaten*

J' .... faire plus de sport.
I'm trying to do ....

Il vient de partir.
He .... left.

'Venir de' + infinitive =
'to have ....'.

Depuis

'Depuis' means ______ or ______.
It's used with the present tense for actions that are ______.

.... depuis 2015.
He's lived in Leeds .... 2015.

Je travaille .... depuis quatre mois.
I've worked as a lawyer .... four months.

Questions

Swap the ______ and the ______ to form a question.
Put a hyphen between the ______ and ______.

.... le français?
Do you like French?

If the ______ ends in a vowel and the ______ starts with a vowel, add a ____.

.... mal au ventre?
Has she got a ....?

Second Go: ...../...../.....

More About the Present Tense

Infinitives

When ____ verbs are ____, the ____ verb stays in the ____.

____ *I want to help other people.*

Not ____ can be followed ____ by an ____ — some need a ____.

These verbs need ____ before ____:

____ *to begin*

____ *to learn*

____ *to succeed*

____ *to succeed in / to manage*

These verbs need ____ before ____:

____ *to try*

____ *to decide*

____ *to stop (oneself)*

____ *to threaten*

____ *She starts listening.*

____ *I'm trying to do more sport.*

____ *He has just left.*

'..........................' + ... = 'to have just done something'.

Depuis

'Depuis' means ____ or ____.
It's used with the present tense for ____ that are ____.

____ *He's lived in Leeds since 2015.*

____ *I've worked as a lawyer for four months.*

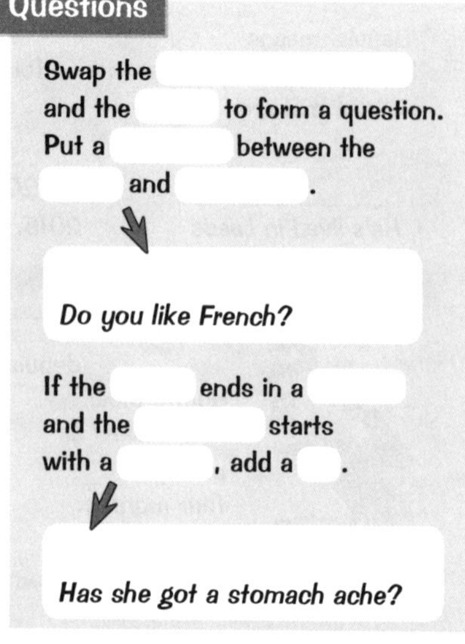

Questions

Swap the ____ and the ____ to form a question.
Put a ____ between the ____ and ____.

____ *Do you like French?*

If the ____ ends in a ____ and the ____ starts with a ____, add a ____.

____ *Has she got a stomach ache?*

Talking About the Future

First Go: ..... /..... /.....

Immediate future tense

The immediate future describes something that is ____________.

Immediate future tense = ________ tense of '______' ('to go') + ________

Il ...... déménager la semaine prochaine.
He is going to ....

Les animaux .... disparaître.
The animals are going ....

Simple future tense

The simple future describes something that ____________.

Most verbs in the simple future tense use ____________ with these endings added:

je	
tu	-as
il/elle/on	
nous	
vous	-ez
ils/elles	

je ....
I will play

nous ....
we will finish

elles ....
they will look

Il .... des chaussures vertes.
He will buy ....

Verbs ending in ______ drop the final ____ before adding the endings:

tu perdras
you ....

elle ....
she will take

Ils .... les fruits.
They will sell the fruit.

Irregular future tense stems

Verb	Stem
	ir-
être	
avoir	

Verb	Stem
faire	
	verr-
devoir	

Verb	Stem
venir	
	voudr-
	pourr-

Verb	Stem
	recevr-
savoir	
falloir	

J'irai à Bordeaux ....
I .... *to Bordeaux tomorrow.*

Vous recevrez une lettre ....
You .... *soon.*

Second Go:
..... /..... /.....

Talking About the Future

Immediate future tense

The immediate future describes ______.

Immediate future tense = ______ + ______

He is going to move house next week.

The animals are going to disappear.

Simple future tense

The simple future describes ______.

______ verbs in the simple future tense use ______ with these endings added:

je	
tu	
il/elle/on	
nous	
vous	
ils/elles	

I will play

we will finish

they will look

He will buy some green shoes.

Verbs ending in ______ drop ______ before ______:

you will lose

she will take

They will sell the fruit.

Irregular future tense stems

Verb	Stem
aller	
être	
avoir	

Verb	Stem
faire	
voir	
devoir	

Verb	Stem
venir	
vouloir	
pouvoir	

Verb	Stem
recevoir	
savoir	
falloir	

I will go to Bordeaux tomorrow.

You will receive a letter soon.

Mixed Practice Quizzes

You know the drill by now — have a go at these quizzes covering p.157-164.
Don't be tempted to look up the answers until you've had a proper go at the quiz.

Quiz 1

Date: ...... / ...... / ......

1) How do you form the immediate future tense in French?
2) Explain the difference between 'devoir' and 'les devoirs'.
3) Give the present tense endings for regular '-ir' verbs.
4) What should you do to the subject pronoun and the verb to form a question in the present tense?
5) Translate into English: 'Elles habitent à La Rochelle depuis 2018.'
6) Give the simple future tense stems for these verbs: 'avoir', 'faire', 'vouloir'.
7) List the forms of 'aller' in the present tense.
8) True or false? The verb 'devoir' is followed by 'de' when it appears before an infinitive.
9) Complete the list of simple future tense forms of 'pouvoir': 'je pourrai', 'tu pourras'...
10) Translate into French: 'We are learning to swim.'

Total:

Quiz 2

Date: ...... / ...... / ......

1) Translate into English: 'Les filles vont travailler dur.'
2) How do you find the stem of a regular verb in the present tense?
3) What does 'venir de' plus an infinitive mean in English?
4) Translate into French: 'We will buy some milk.'
5) What is the French infinitive of the verb 'to make / do'?
6) Put this sentence into the present tense: 'J'irai en vacances.'
7) List the forms of 'être' in the present tense.
8) Translate into French: 'We are going to go jogging.'
9) Give two French verbs that need 'à' before an infinitive is added.
10) Complete the list of forms of 'savoir' in the present tense: 'je sais', 'tu sais'...

Total:

Mixed Practice Quizzes

Quiz 3

Date: ...... / ...... / ......

1) What is different about the simple future stems of '-re' verbs?
2) Complete the list of forms of 'avoir' in the present tense: 'j'ai', 'tu as'...
3) Translate into English: 'Aimez-vous boire du chocolat chaud?'
4) Give two ways you could translate this sentence into English: 'Nous allons au centre-ville.'
5) List the forms of 'vouloir' in the simple future tense.
6) Put this sentence into the simple future tense: 'Vous vendez du pain.'
7) Give the present tense endings for regular '-re' verbs.
8) True or false? In the present tense, 'depuis' is used for actions that are still happening.
9) Translate into French: 'He is trying to leave.'
10) Put this sentence into the present tense: 'On prendra le train.'

Total:

Quiz 4

Date: ...... / ...... / ......

1) Translate into French: 'I have just arrived.'
2) Put this sentence into the immediate future tense: 'Ils jouent ensemble.'
3) What are the two ways 'depuis' can be translated into English?
4) How do you form the simple future tense of regular verbs in French?
5) Explain when you would add a 't' between a verb and a pronoun in a question.
6) Explain the difference between 'savoir' and 'connaître'.
7) Complete the list of forms of 'finir' in the simple future tense: 'je finirai', 'tu finiras'...
8) Translate into French: 'I will go to the park next weekend.'
9) Give the present tense endings for regular '-er' verbs.
10) List the forms of 'devoir' in the present tense.

Total:

Talking About the Past

First Go: ..... / ..... / .....

Perfect tense

The perfect tense describes actions that ________ and ________ in the past.

Perfect tense = ________ tense of 'avoir' ('to ________') or 'être' ('to ____') + Past ________

Verbs that use 'avoir'

____ verbs use the ________ tense of 'avoir' to form the perfect tense.

j'ai	il/elle/on a	vous ____
tu ____	nous ____	ils/elles ont

Past ________ = verb ____ + endings:

'-er' verbs = '....'
regard- → ....

'-ir' verbs = '....'
fin- → ....

'-re' verbs = '....'
vend- → ....

Elle a .... au rugby.
She .... *played rugby. / She played rugby.*

Past .... with 'avoir' don't .... to agree with the ....

Ils ont .... un chat.
.... *bought a cat. /* .... *bought a cat.*

Nous .... nos chausettes.
We .... *lost our* .... *. / We lost our* .... *.*

You don't always need the ________ in English.

Irregular past participles

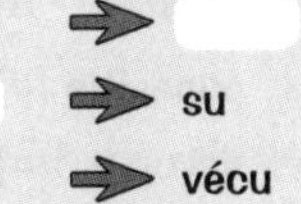

avoir	→ ____	____	→ écrit	____	→ pu
____	→ bu	____	→ été	prendre	→ ____
connaître	→ ____	faire	→ ____	____	→ su
devoir	→ ____	____	→ lu	____	→ vécu
____	→ dit	mettre	→ ____	voir	→ ____

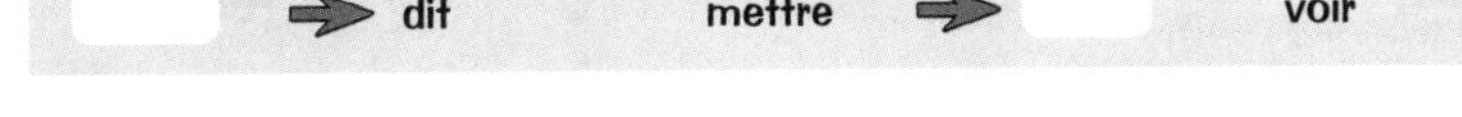

Second Go: ...../...../.....

Talking About the Past

Perfect tense

The perfect tense describes actions that .

Perfect tense = +

Verbs that use 'avoir'

verbs use the of 'avoir' to .

j'ai		

Past = + :

'-er' verbs = regard- →

'-ir' verbs = fin- →

'-re' verbs = vend- →

She has played rugby. / She played rugby.

Past .... with 'avoir' don't .... to agree with the ....

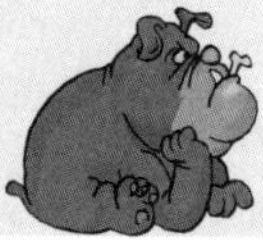

They've bought a cat. / They bought a cat.

We have lost our socks. / We lost our socks.

← You need the in English.

Irregular past participles

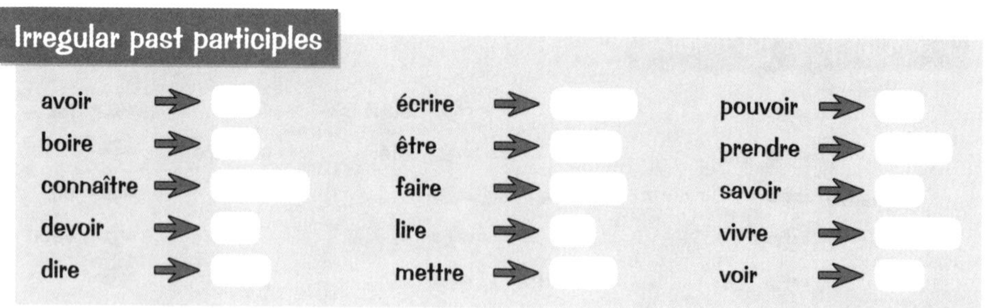

Talking About the Past

First Go: ..... /..... /.....

Verbs that use 'être'

These verbs use the ____ tense of 'être' to form the perfect tense:

je suis	il/elle/on ____	vous êtes
tu es	nous ____	ils/elles ____

aller	____	____	*to go down*	____	*to fall*
venir	____	monter	____	retourner	____
____	*to come back*	____	*to be born*	entrer	____
____	*to arrive*	mourir	____	____	*to go back*
partir	____	____	*to become*		
____	*to go out*	____	*to stay*		

Bilal ____ tôt.
Bilal came early.

Il ____ habillé.
He got dressed.

____ verbs use 'être' in the perfect tense.

Agreement

Verbs that use 'être' must agree with the ____ and ____ of their ____.

Feminine	Plural	Feminine + Plural
Add ____	Add ____	Add ____

Elle ____ au travail.
She has returned to ____.

Les filles ____ il y a une heure.
The girls left ____.

For ____ verbs, the 'être' part goes ____ the ____ pronoun and the past ____.

Ils ____ dans la rivière.
They washed themselves ____.

Agreement with direct objects

Past ____ with 'avoir' change to ____ if there's a direct object or a direct object ____ before the verb.

J'ai mangé la pomme qu'il ____.
I ____ that he recommended.

Les voix que j'____.
The ____ that I heard.

Second Go: ...../...../.....

Talking About the Past

Verbs that use 'être'

verbs use the of 'être' to form the perfect tense:

je suis		

to go
to come
to come back
to arrive
to leave
to go out

to go down
to go up
to be born
to die
to become
to stay

to fall
to return
to go in
to go back

Bilal came early.

He got dressed.

verbs use in the perfect tense.

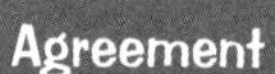

Agreement

Verbs that use must with the and of their subject.

Feminine	Plural	Feminine + Plural

She has returned to work.

The girls left an hour ago.

For verbs, the 'être' part goes the and the .

They washed themselves in the river.

Agreement with direct objects

Past with 'avoir' if there's a direct object or a before the verb.

I ate the apple that he recommended.

The voices that I heard.

Talking About the Past

First Go: ...../...../.....

Imperfect tense

Take the present tense form and remove to find the imperfect stem.

Verb	Stem
	all-
avoir	

Verb	Stem
	parl-
venir	

Then add the :

je		nous	-ions
tu	-ais	vous	
il/elle/on		ils/elles	

Descriptions in the past

The imperfect tense can describe or in the past.

Il .... froid.
It was ....

It can say what for when the action was .

Il .... à l'artiste.
He was talking ....

Je .... quand le téléphone a sonné.
I was reading .... the telephone ....

Être

'Être' is in the imperfect:

j'	nous
tu étais	vous
il/elle/on	ils/elles étaient

C' .... formidable.
It was ....

Things that used to happen

Use the imperfect tense to talk about what you do.

J'allais au parc ....
I .... to the park every day.

Quand j' .... dix ans,
je jouais ....
When I was ten,
I .... the guitar.

is in the as it's describing someone.

Imperfect + 'depuis'

Use the imperfect plus 'depuis' to say what happening.

Il pleuvait depuis ....
It .... for two hours.

Il attendait depuis ....
....
He .... since 6:30 in the morning.

Second Go:
..... /..... /.....

Talking About the Past

Imperfect tense

Take the and to find the imperfect stem.

Verb	Stem
aller	
avoir	

Verb	Stem
parler	
venir	

Then add the :

je		nous	
tu		vous	
il/elle/on		ils/elles	

Descriptions in the past

The imperfect tense can in the past.

It was cold.

It can say what for when the action .

He was talking to the artist.

I was reading when the telephone rang.

Things that used to happen

Use the imperfect tense to talk about what you .

I used to go to the park every day.

When I was ten, I used to play the guitar.

is in the as it's .

Être

'Être' is irregular in the imperfect:

il/elle/on était	

It was great.

Imperfect + 'depuis'

Use the imperfect plus 'depuis' to say .

It had been raining for two hours.

He had been waiting since 6:30 in the morning.

Mixed Practice Quizzes

What's that? You just can't wait to get stuck into another quartet of quizzes? Thought so. Just for you, here are quizzes covering p.167-172 — enjoy.

Quiz 1

Date: ...... / ...... / ......

1) Translate into French: 'We have bought a car.'
2) Complete the list of forms of 'être' in the imperfect tense: 'j'étais', 'tu étais'...
3) Give the past participles for 'avoir', 'être' and 'faire'.
4) Translate into English: 'Elle a acheté trop de bonbons.'
5) Translate into French: 'He came back late.'
6) Which past tense should you use to describe the weather in the past?
7) Do reflexive verbs take 'avoir' or 'être' in the perfect tense?
8) Translate into English: 'J'attendais depuis cinq heures du soir.'
9) When should a past participle that uses 'avoir' change to agree with its subject?
10) Give four verbs that use 'être' in the perfect tense.

Total:

Quiz 2

Date: ...... / ...... / ......

1) How do you form the past participle of regular '-ir' verbs?
2) Explain how past participles for verbs that use 'être' change if the subject is feminine singular.
3) What is the past participle for 'prendre'?
4) Translate into French: 'He has played basketball.'
5) 'Dû' is the past participle of which French verb?
6) Translate into English: 'Ils ont mangé au restaurant hier.'
7) Which tense do you use to talk about something you used to do?
8) Translate into English: 'Il faisait chaud depuis huit heures.'
9) How do you say 'it was' in French?
10) Give the French infinitives for 'to be born' and 'to die'.

Total:

Mixed Practice Quizzes

Quiz 3

Date: ...... / ...... / ......

1) Translate into English: 'Quand j'étais jeune, je voulais changer le monde.'
2) Give the French infinitives for 'to go up' and 'to go down'.
3) True or false? Past participles for regular '-re' verbs end in '-é'.
4) Translate into French: 'He was speaking to his mother.'
5) Give the past participles for 'lire', 'pouvoir' and 'voir'.
6) How do you find the imperfect stem of a French verb?
7) Explain how past participles for verbs that use 'être' change if the subject is plural.
8) Translate into English: 'Nous voyagions depuis plus d'une semaine.'
9) True or false? For reflexive verbs in the perfect tense, the reflexive pronoun goes after the 'être' part.
10) How do you say 'it was raining' in French?

Total:

Quiz 4

Date: ...... / ...... / ......

1) Explain how the perfect tense is formed in French.
2) Translate into French: 'I used to play the drums.'
3) True or false? More verbs use 'être' than 'avoir' in the perfect tense.
4) Give five verbs that use 'avoir' in the perfect tense.
5) Give the imperfect tense stems for 'venir' and 'avoir'.
6) Translate into French: 'She got up at seven o'clock.'
7) What are the past participles for 'mettre' and 'vivre'?
8) Give two ways you could translate this sentence into English: 'J'ai perdu ma pomme.'
9) Give the French infinitives for 'to leave' and 'to go out'.
10) True or false? The imperfect plus 'depuis' is used to say what 'had been' happening.

Total:

Reflexive Verbs and Pronouns

First Go: ..... / ..... / .....

Reflexive pronouns

Reflexive verbs describe actions done to ______.

They need a reflexive ______ which matches the ______ the action.

Myself		Ourselves	
Yourself (inf. sing.)	te	Yourselves (pl., form.)	vous
Himself/herself/itself/oneself		Themselves/each other	

Common reflexive verbs

se laver	______	______	*to argue*
______	*to get up*	______	*to be called*
______	*to go to bed*	se plaindre	______
se détendre	______	s'intéresser à	______
se sentir	______	______	*to enjoy oneself*

In the ______, imperfect and ______ tenses, the reflexive ______ goes between the ______ and the verb.

Nous .... intéressons au cricket.
We are .... in cricket.

Je .... à cinq heures.
I get up at ....

Perfect tense

Reflexive verbs all take ______ in the perfect tense.

Je .... à huit heures.
I had a wash at ....

The past ______ must agree with the ______.

Elle ....
She washed herself.

Immediate future tense

The reflexive ______ goes after the present tense form of ______.

Je .... coucher.
I'm going to go to bed.

The reflexive ______ needs the ______ that matches the subject.

Ils vont se plaindre.
They are .....

Second Go: ...../...../.....

Reflexive Verbs and Pronouns

Reflexive pronouns

Reflexive verbs describe .
They need a which matches the .

Myself		Ourselves	
Yourself (inf. sing.)		Yourselves (pl., form.)	
Himself/herself/itself/oneself		Themselves/each other	

Common reflexive verbs

to wash oneself
to get up
to go to bed
to relax
to feel
to argue
to be called
to complain
to be interested in
to enjoy oneself

In the , and ,
the reflexive goes between the and the .

We are interested in cricket.

I get up at five o'clock.

Perfect tense

Reflexive verbs all
in the perfect tense.

I had a wash at eight o'clock.

The past must
with the .

She washed herself.

Immediate future tense

The reflexive goes
the tense form of .

I'm going to go to bed.

The reflexive needs the
that matches the .

They are going to complain.

Negative Forms

First Go: ..... /..... /.....

Ne...pas

'Ne' and 'pas' go of a verb to make a sentence mean .

Je suis d'accord.
I ....

Je ne suis pas d'accord.
I ....

In the perfect tense, 'ne' and 'pas' go around the bit of or .

Je .... l'école primaire.
I did not like the ....

'Ne' and 'pas' both go infinitives.

Il .... de son fils.
He prefers not to talk about ....

Other negatives

ne...jamais

nothing

no more / no longer

ne...personne /

ne...ni...ni

only / nothing but

Je à York.	I don't go to York any more.
Il ici.	There is nothing .
Je ne vais jamais .	I to the dentist.
Il n'y a personne .	There is better.
Je ne vais ni à Paris ni à Lille.	I to Paris to Lille.
Elle 'un foulard.	She only has one .

Articles

After a negative, 'un', ' ', 'du', ' ' and 'des' usually become ' '.

Elle n'a pas .... sœurs.
She .... *any* ....

Je ne veux .... argent.
I .... *any more money.*

Second Go: ...../...../.....

Negative Forms

Ne...pas

'Ne' and 'pas' go ______ verb to make a sentence ______.

I agree. → *I do not agree.*

In the ______ tense, 'ne' and 'pas' go ______ ______.

'Ne' and 'pas' both go ______ ______.

I did not like the primary school.

He prefers not to talk about his son.

Other negatives

______ *never*

______ *nothing*

______ *no more / no longer*

______ *nobody / anyone*

______ *neither...nor*

______ *only / nothing but*

	I don't go to York any more.
	There is nothing here.
	I never go to the dentist.
	There is nobody better.
	I neither go to Paris nor to Lille.
	She only has one scarf.

Articles

After a negative, ______, ______, ______, ______ and ______ usually become ______.

She doesn't have any sisters.

I don't want any more money.

Would, Could, Should

First Go: ..... /..... /.....

The conditional

Conditional = __________ tense stem + __________ tense ending

Verb			Conditional
manger		je mangeais	je mangerais (I __________)
	il finira		il finirait (he __________)
vendre		nous vendions	nous vendrions (we __________)
	elles seront		elles seraient (they __________)

______ + the __________ tense is always followed by the conditional.

.... j'étais riche, je voyagerais ....
If I were rich, I .... around the world.

To say 'could', use __________ in the conditional plus an __________ .

Elle .... aller .... France.
She could go to France.

To say 'should', use __________ in the conditional plus an __________ .

Tu .... te plaindre.
You should ....

Vouloir

il/elle/on voudrait
vous voudriez

'vouloir' = ...

Je .... aller à l'hôpital.
I would like to go to ....

Aimer

tu aimerais
ils/elles aimeraient

'aimer' = ...

Nous .... aller à la plage.
We would like to go to ....

Second Go: ..... /..... /.....

Would, Could, Should

The conditional

Conditional = ______ + ______

Verb			Conditional
	je mangerai		(I would eat)
	il finira		(he would finish)
	nous vendrons		(we would sell)
	elles seront		(they would be)

______ + the imperfect tense is always ______.

If I were rich, I would travel around the world.

To say 'could', use ______ in the ______ plus ______.

She could go to France.

To say 'should', use ______ in the ______ plus ______.

You should complain.

il/elle/on voudrait

...... = 'to want'

I would like to go to the hospital.

j'aimerais

...... = 'to like'

We would like to go to the beach.

Giving Orders

First Go: ..... / ..... / .....

Imperatives

Imperatives give an ______ or ______.

They use the 'tu', ______ and ______ forms of a ______ tense verb.

'tu' form (inf. sing.)	Sors!	
'nous' form		Let's get out!
'vous' form (pl., form)		Get out!

Don't use subject .... with the imperative.

Irregular imperatives

'Tu' forms that end in ______ lose the final ______. This includes regular ______ verbs.

.... Jean-Paul!
Look at Jean-Paul!

.... de me parler!
Stop talking to ....!

Some verbs have ______ imperatives:

Imperative form	être	avoir	savoir	aller
tu	sois			va
			sachons	
	soyez	ayez		

Only the .... form of 'aller' has an .... imperative.

Negative and reflexive imperatives

Add ______ before the verb and ______ after it to make an imperative ______.

.... écoute ....!
Don't ....!

.... vendez .... le poisson!
Don't .... the ....!

Imperative reflexive verbs need an ______ pronoun after the verb.

______, imperative reflexive verbs use the normal ______ pronouns.

Lève-........!
Get up!

Asseyons-........!
Let's ....!

.... lève ....!
Don't get up!

Second Go:
...../...../.....

Giving Orders

Imperatives

Imperatives give .
They use the , and forms of a verb.

'tu' form (inf. sing.)		Get out!
'nous' form		
'vous' form (pl., form)		

Don't use .... with the ....

Irregular imperatives

forms that end in lose the final . This includes verbs.

Look at Jean-Paul!

Stop talking to me!

Some verbs have :

Imperative form	être	avoir	savoir	aller
tu				
nous				
vous				

Only the ...... form of .... has an .... imperative.

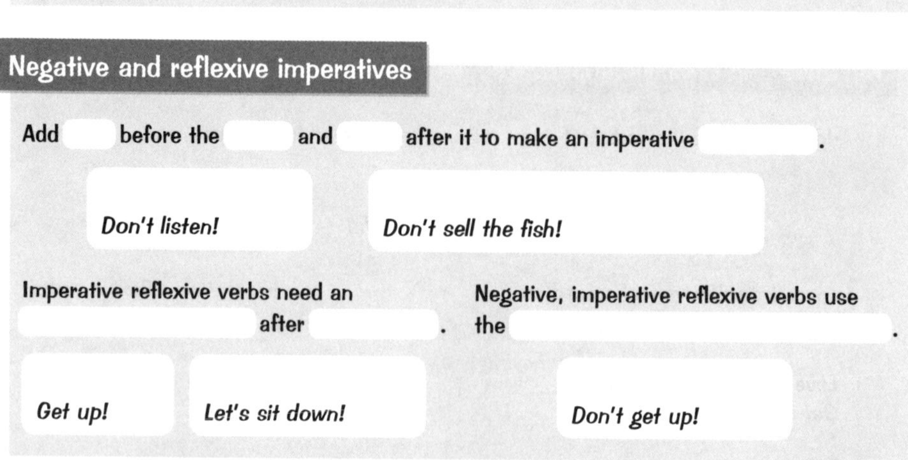

Negative and reflexive imperatives

Add before the and after it to make an imperative .

Don't listen!

Don't sell the fish!

Imperative reflexive verbs need an after .

Negative, imperative reflexive verbs use the .

Get up!

Let's sit down!

Don't get up!

'Had done' and '-ing'

First Go: ..... /..... /.....

The pluperfect tense

Use the pluperfect tense for saying what you ______ in the past.

Pluperfect = ______ tense of '______' + Past ______

J' .... une lettre.
I had written a letter.

Elles ....
They had argued.

Present participles

Present participle = ______ stem + ______

Verb	______ stem	Present Participle
	regard-	______ (*watching*)
finir		______ (*finishing*)
	vend-	vendant (______)
faire		______ (*doing / making*)

Don't use a present participle in place of the .... tense.
'I like doing...' = 'J'aime ....'

Irregular present participles:
être = ...
.... = ayant
.... = sachant

Renonçant à l'idée, Clare est ....
.... *the idea, Clare returned home.*

'En' + present participle means '______ / ______ doing something'.

Il .... le journal en déjeunant.
He reads the paper ....

J' .... en sachant les faits.
I succeeded .... *the facts.*

Perfect infinitives

'Avoir' or ______ + past ______ means '______ something'.

Il .... d'avoir joué au foot.
He regrets .... *football.*

Après .... en Italie, elle voudrait aller en Espagne.
After having been to Italy, she ....

The .... must agree for .... verbs.

Second Go: ..... /..... /.....

'Had done' and '-ing'

The pluperfect tense

Use the pluperfect tense for saying what you ____________ .

Pluperfect = ____________ + ____________

I had written a letter.

They had argued.

Present participles

Present participle = ____________ + ____________

Verb		Present Participle
		(watching)
		(finishing)
		(selling)
		(doing / making)

Don't use a present participle in place of the .... tense.
'I like doing...' =
' .... '

Irregular present participles:
être = ...
avoir = ...
savoir = ...

Giving up on the idea, Clare returned home.

____ + present participle means ____________ .

He reads the paper while having lunch.

I succeeded by knowing the facts.

Perfect infinitives

____ or ____ + past participle means ____________ .

He regrets having played football.

After having been to Italy, she would like to go to Spain.

The .... must .... for .... verbs.

The Passive

First Go: ..... / ..... / .....

The present passive

In a passive sentence, the subject ______ to it.

Present passive = Present tense of ______ + Past ______

Il .... aidé par ses parents.
He is helped ....

The ______ must agree.

La télé réalité .... par beaucoup de gens.
.... *is watched by* ....

The past and future passives

The passive is formed in ______ way in different tenses.
The ______ part changes into the ______ .

Perfect Passive	La photo a été prise.	The photo ______ .
Imperfect Passive	Le livre était écrit pendant la guerre.	The book ______ during ______ .
Future Passive	Les déchets seront jetés.	The rubbish ______ .

Using 'on'

The passive isn't used very much in French.
French speakers often use ______ with an ______ sentence instead.

.... vu l'homme.
We didn't see .... /
.... *wasn't seen.*

.... une nouvelle planète.
We discovered a .... /
A .... *was discovered.*

Second Go:
..... /..... /.....

The Passive

The present passive

In a passive sentence, the subject ______.

Present passive = ______ + ______

He is helped by his parents.

The ______ must ______.

Reality TV is watched by lots of people.

The past and future passives

The passive is formed in the ______ in ______ tenses.
The ______ changes into the ______.

Perfect Passive	La photo a été prise.	
Imperfect Passive	Le livre était écrit pendant la guerre.	
Future Passive	Les déchets seront jetés.	

Using 'on'

The passive ______ in French.
French speakers often ______ with an ______.

We didn't see the man. / The man wasn't seen.

We discovered a new planet. / A new planet was discovered.

Impersonal Verbs and the Subjunctive

First Go: ..... / ..... / .....

Impersonal verbs

Impersonal verbs always have ____ as their ____.

____ *it's about*

il est nécessaire de ____

il semble ____

____ *it's raining*

____ *you must / it's necessary to*

____ *it's snowing*

il fait chaud / froid ____ / ____

.... une mère et ses enfants.
It's about a ....

.... argent.
It's a question of ....

Use 'il est nécessaire de' and 'il faut' with ____.

Il est nécessaire de .... contre le racisme.
.... *to fight against* ....

Il faut .... au lycée.
You must go ....

The subjunctive

The subjunctive is used after some ____ verbs and some ____. There's often ____ in English.

You need to recognise these subjunctive forms:

____	____	____	____	____
j'aie	je sois	je fasse	j'aille	je puisse
tu aies	tu sois	tu fasses	tu ailles	tu puisses
il/elle/on ait	il/elle/on soit	il/elle/on fasse	il/elle/on aille	il/elle/on puisse
nous ayons	nous soyons	nous fassions	nous allions	nous puissions
vous ayez	vous soyez	vous fassiez	vous alliez	vous puissiez
ils/elles aient	ils/elles soient	ils/elles fassent	ils/elles aillent	ils/elles puissent

These expressions are followed by the subjunctive:

Il faut que tu fasses la vaisselle.
.... *the washing-up.*

Il est nécessaire que vous soyez sages.
It is necessary that ....

Bien qu'elle ait deux enfants...
.... *two children...*

Avant que vous partiez...
Before ....*...*

Second Go: ..... /..... /.....

Impersonal Verbs and the Subjunctive

Impersonal verbs

Impersonal verbs always have as .

it's about

it seems

you must / it's necessary to

it's necessary to

it's raining

it's snowing

/ *it's hot / cold*

It's about a mother and her children.

It's a question of money.

Use 'il est ' and with .

It is necessary to fight against racism.

You must go to school.

The subjunctive

The subjunctive is used after and

. There's often in English.

You need to recognise these subjunctive forms:

j'aie	je sois	je fasse	j'aille	je puisse
tu aies	tu sois	tu fasses	tu ailles	tu puisses
il/elle/on ait	il/elle/on soit	il/elle/on fasse	il/elle/on aille	il/elle/on puisse
nous ayons	nous soyons	nous fassions	nous allions	nous puissions
vous ayez	vous soyez	vous fassiez	vous alliez	vous puissiez
ils/elles aient	ils/elles soient	ils/elles fassent	ils/elles aillent	ils/elles puissent

These are followed by the subjunctive:

Il faut que tu fasses la vaisselle.

Il est nécessaire que vous soyez sages.

Bien qu'elle ait deux enfants...

Avant que vous partiez...

Mixed Practice Quizzes

That's right, time for the final round of quizzes — don't say we don't spoil you. Each quiz is filled with ten juicy questions to test the content from p.175-188.

Quiz 1

Date: ...... / ...... / ......

1) How do you form the conditional in French?
2) Complete the list of French reflexive pronouns: 'me', 'te'...
3) What do you use the pluperfect tense to talk about?
4) Translate into English: 'Il n'y a plus de foulards.'
5) True or false? You must include the subject pronoun when giving orders.
6) Translate into English: 'Je suis aidé par ma sœur.'
7) How do you say 'it is necessary to' in French?
8) What negative phrase means 'never' in French?
9) Which stem should you use to form a present participle?
10) How do you say 'I would be' in French?

Total:

Quiz 2

Date: ...... / ...... / ......

1) Translate into English: 'Nous nous sentirions mieux.'
2) Make this order negative: 'Ouvrez la porte!'
3) Translate into French: 'It's about two children.'
4) True or false? The present participle is used to form the passive.
5) Translate into English:
   'S'il avait plus d'argent, il pourrait acheter ces chaussures.'
6) True or false? The passive is frequently used in French.
7) Add 'ne' and 'pas' to the following sentence to make it negative:
   'Tu as vu mon chien.'
8) Give the phrase 'ils se disputent' in the pluperfect tense.
9) Translate into French: 'Let's go to the shops!'
10) What does 'il semble' mean in English?

Total:

Mixed Practice Quizzes

Quiz 3

Date: ...... / ...... / ......

1) Translate into French: 'I regret having gone to the café.'
2) Explain what's wrong with this sentence: 'Clara s'est levé tôt.'
3) How do you say 'I have nothing' in French?
4) What does the following mean in English? 'Après avoir écrit la lettre...'
5) What is special about the form of 'être' used in this sentence? 'Il faut que tu sois sage.'
6) Translate into French: 'We should travel around the world.'
7) Turn this sentence into an order: 'Tu parles à Marc plus tard.'
8) Translate into English: 'Les magazines seront vendus.'
9) Translate into French: 'I go to bed at 11 o'clock.'
10) Put the following sentence into the conditional: 'Ils veulent aller à la plage.'

Total:

Quiz 4

Date: ...... / ...... / ......

1) Give the three imperative forms of the verb 'avoir'.
2) 'Puisse' is a subjunctive form of which French verb?
3) Translate into English: 'Le livre était prise il y a trente ans.'
4) How do you say 'while finishing my homework' in French?
5) Turn this sentence into an order: 'Vous vous asseyez.'
6) What does this sentence mean in English? 'Je ne veux qu'une tranche de gâteau.'
7) What does 'je vendrais' mean in English?
8) Translate into French: 'They had wanted two cats.'
9) Impersonal verbs always begin with which subject pronoun?
10) Translate into English: 'Il n'y avait personne au cinéma.'

Total:

FANR41